W9-CNP-145

This is the DACHSHUND

By **LEONORE LOEB ADLER,**
based on Dr. Fritz Engelmann's **DER DACHSHUND**

second (revised) edition

Distributed in the U.S.A. by T.F.H. Publications, Inc., 211 West Sylvania Avenue, P.O. Box 27, Neptune City, N.J. 07753; in England by T.F.H. (Gt. Britain) Ltd., 13 Nutley Lane, Reigate, Surrey; in Canada to the book store and library trade by Clarke, Irwin & Company, Clarwin House, 791 St. Clair Avenue West, Toronto 10, Ontario; in Canada to the pet trade by Rolf C. Hagen Ltd., 3225 Sartelon Street, Montreal 382, Quebec; in Southeast Asia by Y.W. Ong, 9 Lorong 36 Geylang, Singapore 14; in Australia and the south Pacific by Pet Imports Pty. Ltd., P.O. Box 149, Brookvale 2100, N.S.W., Australia. Published by T.F.H. Publications Inc. Ltd., The British Crown Colony of Hong Kong.

Cover Photo: "Midnight"; international prizewinning photograph of v. Hohenhorst's Georgie Girl-M, at the age of two months. Photo by Milton M. Laemle.

Frontispiece: My family; *All the Adlers:* Beverly; Barry with wife, Karen; Helmut; Leonore with "Bella"; and Evelyn. Photo by Irving Fine.

ISBN #0-87666-278-5

© 1975 by T.F.H. Publications, Inc. Ltd.

Published by T.F.H. Publications, Inc. Ltd., The British Crown Colony of Hong Kong. Manufactured in Hong Kong.

CONTENTS

DEDICATION

To "Bella, my bestest"
(De Sangpur Wee Bell of the Ball)
with tender love

Leonore Loeb Adler.
Photo by Carol Studios.

VITA

Leonore Loeb Adler was born in Karlsruhe, Germany. She was educated there and in Berlin, as well as in Lausanne, Switzerland. In Switzerland her uncle's and aunt's Miniature Dachshund introduced her to the breed.

She came to the United States in 1938 where she was married in 1943. With her husband, Dr. Helmut E. Adler, and their three children, Barry, Beverly, and Evelyn, her unwavering attention was always focused on Dachshunds, not only in the United States but also in other countries.

The author lives most of the time in Jamaica, New York, but spends weekends and vacations in her "retreat" in Rhode Island. She and her husband run a small Miniature Dachshund kennel, "Von Hohenhorst."

Mrs. Adler belongs to several Dachshund clubs. She was chairman of the Dachshund Club of America's Miniature Dachshund Committee for nine years and president of the National Miniature Dachshund Club for several years; she edited the N.M.D.C. Miniature Dachshund Digest *for six years. Today she is an officer of the N.M.D.C. in the capacity of secretary.*

Her manifold interests include the fields of psychology and archeology. She is a research assistant in the Department of Animal Behavior at the American Museum of Natural History in New York, N.Y. In the interval between the time work started on the Second Edition of This Is the Dachshund, *and its publication, Leonore Loeb Adler received her Ph.D. degree in experimental social psychology from Adelphi University, Garden City, N.Y.*

9

FOREWORD

The breeding, rearing and competitive exhibition of purebred dogs constitute a hazardous road with many pitfalls and heartaches along the way. Only true dedication can help smooth the bumps. For those who possess such dedication, the gratification of eventual successful endeavor is satisfaction enough. For those who do not, such success will not come, and they will seek their gratification elsewhere.

Those who are truly dedicated to the production of the perfect Dachshund must possess a perpetual thirst for knowledge. Although we remain aware that perfection can never be achieved, our efforts must not relax lest we slip backward rather than progress forward.

This perpetual thirst can be slowly but never completely slaked by experience, conversation and reading all that is available about the breed so many of us have chosen to promote. Perhaps the written word is most reliable, as experiences tend to fade with time, and that which is learned from conversation often fades even faster. Hence, the pages which follow can be read and re-read to help all those who so choose to absorb that which is presented.

PHILIP S. BISHOP
Former President and current
First Vice-President
The Dachshund Club of America, Inc.

INTRODUCTION

A great big "Howdy" is extended to the new second edition of "This is the Dachshund"! Owners of Dachshunds, Standard and Miniature, will get much pleasure and useful information from this book, with its many pertinent additions and helpful contributions by active Dachshund breeders and enthusiasts. Not only will readers benefit from these pages, but also Dachshunds as a breed—a cause most dear to our hearts, as you all know.

Good luck to the author
from her good friend,
Sid Sims

President of the Dachshund Club of America
February, 1972

Texdox Ragtime Cowboy Joe is shown winning under Judge George Spradling. He is handled by Sid Sims, who is the co-owner with Ann Sims of Texas. This little dog was Best Miniature from the Open Classes at the D.C.A. Specialty Show in California in 1971. Photo by Morry Twomey.

PREFACE

When *This is the Dachshund* was first published in 1966, it was greeted by eager readers. Universally well received with sincere enthusiasm, the book filled a void that had existed for a long time. The need for an informative text was shared equally by the Dachshund fancy in general and breeders, as well as pet owners in particular.

In the first edition of *This is the Dachshund* much of Dr. Fritz Engelmann's original text was left intact, though some parts were deleted completely, while new sections were added here and there. For example, Chapter III was then a completely new addition. In the present and revised second edition, the third chapter remains complete and without any change, because of its importance to breeders. And, as I did previously, my thanks go to Drs. J. P. Scott, the late C. C. Little, and the late T. C. Schneirla for critically reading this chapter on genetics.

While in Chapter I only a small section about the History of Dachshunds remains, a large portion of the history specific to the German Dachshund has been deleted. In its place the following modern, up-to-date contributions were added . . . and at this time I would like to express my appreciation to their authors.

Mrs. Anneliese Wurm of Baden in southern Germany wrote on the status of German Dachshunds and the Deutscher Teckelclub (D.T.K.) regulations for the three sizes: Standard, Miniature, and Rabbit Dachshunds. Her explanations of the dog rating and breeding rules were most informative. Very explicit sections on dog shows and field trials make the present system easily understood by those not familiar with the German regulations. Mrs. Wurm runs her "vom Fürstenfels Kennels" and is breeder-owner-handler of smooth and wirehaired Miniature Dachshunds. She is a member of the D.T.K. and a writer and translator of many informative articles for dog magazines. One of her most frequent topics is genetics, which constitutes one of her major interests.

Mr. Angel Negal of Northants., England, contributed a most thorough discourse on British Dachshunds and goes back 50 years to trace the most important British bloodlines. Since many of these Dachshunds were exported, the tracing of their lineage will be of interest the world over. Mr. Negal is a man of many accomplishments. He has been breeding Dachshunds since 1937 and was a member of the Miniature Dachshund Club's Committee in 1938. Now he is president of the Miniature Dachshund Club, honorary secretary of the Dachshund Council, and chairman of the Eastern Counties Dachshund Association. Mr. Negal edited both the 1966–1968 and 1969–1971 editions of the *Dachshund Club Handbook.* He was the owner of the first smooth champion Miniature Dachshund bitch, who was one of the 33 champions he owned, of which 32 were home-bred. His kennel is identified by the name "Montreux."

While there is no report on Australian Dachshunds, the reader gets a small glimpse of them from the two photos contributed by Mrs. Cassia Jay of Victoria, owner of the small Harca Kennels.

Sarah (Mrs. Irving) Diamond of Quebec, Canada, is one of the most active international supporters and promoters of Dachshunds in general and Miniature Dachshunds specifically. A knowledgeable breeder, handler and exhibitor for many years, she is co-owner with her husband of the successful "Di-Mar Kennels." Currently she is director of the Canadian Kennel Club, after being re-elected to the Board of C.K.C. the fourth time for a two-year term. Mrs. Diamond also is chairman of the Judges' Committee, and chairman of the Registration Committee. She is a judge of the Dachshund breed and member of several Dachshund clubs in both Canada and the United States, namely the Dachshund Club of America and the National Miniature Dachshund Club. She was elected for several years in a row and formerly was serving as a director of the National Miniature Dachshund Club.

Mr. John Hutchinson Cook of New Jersey brought his article on the History of the Dachshund Club of America up to date. While he was president of the D.C.A. (for 13 years) he did much to promote the national interest in this club and in the breed. He helped to further the status of Miniature Dachshunds towards their present popularity. Although Mr. Cook judges other breeds also, he has been a judge of the Dachshund breed since 1946 and has judged almost all regional specialty shows. He owns the "Kleetal Kennels," which are famous for many smooth Standard Dachshund champions.

In Chapter II the newly approved changes of the Dachshund Standard by the American Kennel Club have been incorporated. The most important of these changes concerns Miniature Dachshunds, whose maximum weight is now approved to be under 10 pounds at 12 months old or over.

Many new sections on different topics were added to Chapter IV to discuss current issues not dealt with before. Special thanks, given as follows according to the order of appearance of their articles, are due to the contributors.

Baroness Edita Van der Lyn of Arkansas wrote on ways of preventing the crippling disc problems. She, as stage, screen, and television trainer of Dachshunds, both Miniature and Standard, is well aware of what Dachshunds can and should not do. Though she was born to the title of Baroness, she renounced it when she became an American citizen in 1952, but she uses it still in "showbiz." Mrs. Van der Lyn is a writer for several dog magazines and a member of several dog clubs; her specific club relationship with Dachshunds is to the National Miniature Dachshund Club.

Dr. Robert L. Leighton of California, a veterinarian at the School of Veterinary Medicine, University of California, has good advice for Dachshunds with posterior paralysis. His cart for Dachshunds with the disc problem is easily constructed and gives mobility to the low, long and little patients.

Dr. Boris Levinson of New York is a practicing psychologist who devotes his time to teaching at Yeshiva University, New York, his private practice, and writing books and articles for professional journals.

The next contributor is more than a most conscientious judge and a successful breeder and handler who owns some of the top winning Dachshunds in the United States in all three coats and both sizes. Peggy Westphal of New York is also a good friend, one who came to the rescue on a 24-hour basis. (Literally 24 hours! After the assigned writer on "Grooming" did not come through with the promised article, Peggy jumped in and tackled this important topic perfectly, clearly, in an easy to follow style.) Mrs. Peggy Aldis Westphal is well experienced on this subject, as the reader will quickly realize. Her kennel prefix is "von Westphalen," which can be found in many pedigrees in all three coats. She was a former director of the Dachshund Club of America and presently serves as a director of the National Miniature Dachshund Club.

Jeanne A. Rice of New York contributed an article well worth while for beginners as well as experienced fanciers and breeders. In these days, when it is so easy to travel, her contribution to the book is very valuable. Jeanne Rice is an up-and-coming star in the Dachshund world. Not only is she a successful exhibitor and handler—trained under the able guidance of her father, Thomas J. Rice, a director of the D.C.A.—but also a knowledgeable breeder, with the diligent assistance of her mother, Hilda Rice. Under the kennel prefix "Tori-Jarice Dachshunds" they have produced top-quality Miniature Dachshunds in all three coats. Jeanne Rice belongs to many Dachshund clubs and is currently assistant secretary of the Dachshund Club of America and second vice president of the National Miniature Dachshund Club, as well as chairman of the Trophy Committee of the N.M.D.C.

A clear description of American Dachshund shows was contributed by Mrs. Grace B. Hill (Mrs. William Burr Hill) of Florida, who is the most devoted, tireless, efficient, industrious and capable Dachshundist of all time. (It sounds exaggerated, but it isn't!) Under her kennel prefix of "De Sangpur," and with the constant help of her sister, Mary Gore, she bred, raised and showed Standard and Miniature champions in all three coats; therefore, Mrs. Hill has a full understanding of all the issues facing the breed. Gracie, as she is known to her friends, is involved in Dachshund matters on a regional and local basis as well as on a national level. Through her efforts as secretary of the Dachshund Club of America since 1954, the club runs smoothly and the membership is well informed on all matters concerning Dachshunds. Before that she was a director of the D.C.A. While Grace B. Hill lived on Long Island, New York, she was instrumental in initiating the incorporation of the National Miniature Dachshund Club in 1952 and has been serving as an officer of the club ever since. Presently she is treasurer of the N.M.D.C., to which position she has been elected for the last 11 years. She has always been a staunch supporter of the *N.M.D.C. Miniature Dachshund Digest*, and her ideas and suggestions helped greatly to bring this club magazine to its present high level. Mrs. Hill also helped to organize the Dachshund Association of Long Island in 1950. She was president from 1955 through 1968, when she retired. From an entry of 146 mainly local Dachshunds in 1950, the first specialty show of the club, entries increased in 1968 to 365 Dachshunds from all over the U.S. As of this date, the D.A.L.I. holds the record for Dachshund conformation shows. Then Gracie moved, and her local activities included the Florida dog clubs. She was elected secretary of the Jacksonville Dog Fanciers Association, an all-breed club, and treasurer of the Jacksonville Combined Specialty Clubs.

A helpful and concise article on "handling" was contributed by Hannelore Heller of Illinois, who, besides being a breeder in her own right (together with her husband Joseph she runs the "Han-Jo Kennels"), is one of the top-notch A.K.C.-licensed handlers in the United States. She handles any good Dachshund, regardless of coat, color or size, to the coveted championship and beyond that. Mrs. Heller is a member of the Professional Handlers Guild, the Dachshund Club of America and the National Miniature Dachshund Club.

Her article is followed by one on Junior Handling, written by George C. Wanner of New Jersey, who is one of the busiest Dachshundists I know. He has been a breed judge since 1965 and a field trial judge since 1966. His club activities include serving as director of the Dachshund Club of America (since 1963 to the present), treasurer of the D.C.A. from 1966 to 1968 and D.C.A. Delegate to the American Kennel Club from 1968 to the present, Mr. Wanner is currently chairman of the D.C.A.'s Committee on Junior Handling; besides these activities, he has belonged to the Morris Hills Dog Training Club since 1962 and the Sussex Hills Kennel Club since

1955, holding such varied offices as director, to the present, treasurer, president and chairman of the first point show. His activities for the Dachshund Club of New Jersey are equally as admirable. Mr. Wanner has served as president as well as director since 1959 to the present. Together with Charles Campbell he organized the first Regional Dachshund Club Field Trial for points with A.K.C. approval, which was held in 1967 and has continued each year since. George Wanner and his wife Margaret run "Wanner's Kennels," raising and showing wirehaired Standard Dachshunds.

The most drastic change occurred with Chapter V, dealing with the hunt. Granted that Dachshunds are hounds and meant to go after badger, fox, wild boar, deer and any small game, as well as rabbit, above and below the earth. The German field trials and the training described in Chapter V of the first edition were useful in order to show the potential of a Dachshund and how he performed in actuality. However, none of the English-speaking countries give such rigorous field trial training and tests. Therefore I deemed it more beneficial to Dachshunds and their owners to present more about the existing opportunities to train and test Dachshunds in areas specifically related to the work for which they were originally bred.

Three types of work suitable to the versatile Dachshund can be pursued: (1) obedience training and testing, (2) field trial experience, and (3) the newest sport, Dachshund racing. It was because of such thinking, as described above, that the three articles have been added, one for each type of work, written by an expert in the specific area. My sincere thanks for their contributions go to all three Dachshund enthusiasts. In order of the appearance of their contributions, they are:

Arnold L. Korn, O.D. of Tennessee, wrote the most clearly understood and easiest to follow outline of how a beginner should go about Obedience Training. His success, with his own Miniature Dachshunds, has been admired for years, not only by Miniature Dachshund owners, but by Standard Dachshund owners as well. Of course in all his endeavors, Dr. Korn was ably assisted by his wife, who also deserves credit for the patient and diligent obedience training of their hounds. His most important accomplishments are that of an A.K.C. Tracking Judge, a Field Representative and a member of the National Association of Dog Obedience Instructors; he is also a member of the Advisory Board and instructor of the Memphis Obedience Training Club; he was formerly president of the Memphis Dachshund Club and is currently a member of the National Miniature Dachshund Club.

The article on Field Trials was written by David C. Mullen, Jr. of Pennsylvania. Not only is he the Dachshund Club of America's third vice president, but he has been a director of the club for the past nine years and is now serving for the 11th year as chairman of D.C.A.'s Field Trial Committee. With his wife, Dot, helping along as D.C.A.'s Field Trial Secretary, very successful and enjoyable field trials have been organized and together they have promoted the interest in Dachshund Field Trials. David Mullen was a former president of the Western Pennsylvania Dachshund Club and is now a director of the club. The Mullens run a small kennel of Standard Dachshunds with the prefix of "Da-Dor," which has produced not only show champions, but field trial champions as well. Ever since their first field trial in 1955, one of their steady interests has been promoting hunting Dachshunds.

The last article in this revised edition of *This is the Dachshund* is a spirited account by a trio of Dachshund racing enthusiasts. Wini and Rod MacLean and Mary Lou Hatcher, all of Oregon, have been partners in the "Running Dog Ranch" for about six years raising Rottweilers and Miniature Dachshunds. Their love for the sport originated in California from where they came. Wini and Rod McLean now concentrate on owning and breeding the dogs, which are mainly Miniature Dachshunds, while Mary Lou Hatcher manages the boarding, training and show kennels as a professional handler. They are all members of the Springfield (Oregon) Kennel Club, where Mary Lou is a director and Wini is treasurer; they belong to several Dachshund clubs on the west coast, as well as to the National Miniature Dachshund Club and the Canadian Miniature Dachshund Club.

My most cordial thanks to all the contributors for sharing so generously of their knowledge and expertise.

Before closing I would like to add that I exchanged practically all the photos shown in the first edition for newer, up-to-date pictures for the second edition. The photos were sent to me by Dachshund owners from all over the United States. Furthermore, I want to express my appreciation to all those who helped collect photos for me; among them were Mrs. Charlie Mays, Mrs. Hannelore Heller, Mrs. Peggy Westphal, and Mrs. Ethel Bigler.

With great pleasure I also want to acknowledge the endorsement of this book's *second and revised edition* received from the Dachshund Club of America's former President and current First Vice-President Philip S. Bishop of Ohio. He was—as judge, owner, exhibitor, and breeder of "Lynsulee" Dachshunds—well aware of the purpose of the book, which is to give a better understanding of the breed, and the message it brings, which is to strive for a more perfect and more proficient Dachshund.

The kind support from the current President of the Dachshund Club of America, Sid Sims of Texas, is sincerely appreciated. A Dachshund enthusiast for many years, Mr. Sims understands the problems and joys connected with breeding and showing Dachshunds. He is a breeder and handler, together with his wife, Ann. The Simses run the "Texdox" kennel of smooths Standard and smooths as well as longhaired Miniature Dachshunds.

I hope that the enthusiasm for the breed is conveyed to the reader as he, or she, progresses through these pages. My best wishes to each, to win a multitude of the coveted gold D.C.A. Dachshund pins. A poem comes to my mind, which my daughter made up for me once; it went like this:

Black-&-Tan and Gold Dachshunds
By Evelyn Renée Adler

Dachshunds, Dachshunds—
running everywhere all over the house,
Dachshunds, Dachshunds—
running all across my mother's blouse.

Perhaps some day this little verse will be appropriate for each reader also. Good luck, success and much enjoyment with your Dachsies!

Leonore Loeb Adler

Jamaica, New York, February, 1972.

Two wirehaired Miniature Dachshunds that are closely related: dam (left) Kinkora's Maid of Flight MW and her son Tori-Jarice's Wee Jethro MW. Both are owned by Hilda B. Rice of New York. Photo by Salvatore J. Miceli.

Three smooth Miniature Dachshund littermates in a creel; von Hohenhorst's Gimli M, owner Grace B. Hill of Florida, and von Hohenhorst's Georgie Girl M as well as Go-Go Girl M, both owned by Leonore Loeb Adler of New York. Photo by Milton M. Laemle.

These two longhaired Miniature Dachshund litter brothers are: (left) Minikin Envoy of Nikobar, co-owned by Barbara J. Nichols of California and Jeanne A. Rice of New York, and Minikin Emissary of Nikobar, owned by Hilda B. Rice of New York. Photo by Salvatore J. Miceli.

Chapter I
History

"Tell me the past, and I will show you the future."

The domesticated dog is descended from the wolf, or possibly from wild canines that were also the ancestors of our present-day wolves. Much time was needed to create the present varieties and the manifold breeds of dogs.

The hounds, with their long dropped ears, originated in west and central Europe. Their earliest representative was the Bracke, the prototype of the hound. Its task was to rouse the game and to drive it through the thicket in the direction of the hunter or toward a trap. Because of the snapping and breaking sound of dried branches and twigs—so one speculation goes—the name "Bracke," or "Brakke," for the hound was originated. Another speculation ventures that such a name found its beginning with the "broken" and crooked legs. And to this day there are certain regions in central Europe where a Dachshund is called a Bracke.

It is believed that from the Bracke developed all later West European hunting dogs (with long and hanging ears), such as Pointers, Setters, Basset Hounds, Bloodhounds, and Dachshunds.

Historically, the developmental stages of the Dachshund were probably the short legs, the ability to follow scent trails, and finally the capacity to hunt underground in dens and warrens. Dr. Schäme concluded, after a study of dog skulls, that there was a close ancestral relationship between Dachshunds and Pinschers. Apparently during the re-establishment of the wirehaired Dachshund, much German Pinscher blood was introduced. Through the offspring of these crossings, Pinscher characteristics appeared in many smooth Dachshund family lines. These similarities misled Dr. Schäme into believing that Pinschers were involved in the origin of the Dachshund.

Other theories of origin can also be traced to erroneous inferences or deductions.

Some, for example, believe that the Dachshund existed 4000 years ago in ancient Egypt.* There is a portrayal of a dog and a hieroglyphic inscription reading "*tekal*" or "*tekar*"† on a monument of Thutmose III. The dog,

---

* See Chapter 3 : Genetics : Descent and Heredity.

† Dr. Max Hilzheimer reported such an inscription on the stela of King Antef who lived some 650 years earlier; but this dog did not resemble any Dachshund. L.L.A.

Westphal's Killer Joe, a Longhaired Miniature Dachshund, is lovingly held by Carrie Westphal. Owner Peggy Westphal. Photo by Allen Westphal.

however, does not have the least similarity to a Dachshund, and the translation rests on the false interpretation of the hieroglyphics. The correct meaning leads to the word "*tqru*," which can be translated into "fiery." Besides this, the erroneous word "*tekal*" has no connection whatsoever to the German word for Dachshund, "*Teckel*." This word is German in origin and evolved from the modifications of various vowels. To illustrate, here is the historical sequence of the German names: *Tachs-Krieger, Tachskriecher, Tachshunt, Dachshund, Dachsel, Dackel, Tackel, Teckel. Dachshund* and *Teckel* are therefore synonyms, somewhat like ass and donkey.

Without doubt, in ancient times and in different countries small dogs of varied appearances were used to pursue small game underground. Only later were definite types of such small dogs bred by deliberate selection; this naturally resulted in substantially different breeds.

As to the history of such "earthdogs" in Germany, it is very questionable whether the beaverhound (*Bibarhunt*), mentioned in the *Lex Bajuvarum*

Dachshunds at work, from "La Vénerie du Jaques du Fouilloux" (1561).

("Law of the Bavarians"), used to hunt beavers, badgers, etc., was an ancestor of the Dachshund. This lawbook of the 5th century A.D. stated, "whoever kills a dog which hunts under the earth and is called Bibarhunt, has to replace him and, in addition, is fined seven solidis."

In 1561, Jaques du Fouilloux in *La Vénerie* ("The Hunt") illustrated earthdogs at work. But these show little resemblance to the Dachshund; in many features they rather resemble the primitive Spaniel. Woodcuts made in 1582 by Jost Ammons portray a badger and rabbit hunt. This is probably the earliest reference to the work of the modern Dachshund. It shows the "Dachshund" with a terrier-pinscher body and docked tail. In 1671 *Ein artig Büchlein von dem Weydwerk und der Falknerey* ("A Good Booklet on Hunting and Falconry") was published. Among other things, it discussed a little dog "for tracking after rabbits; some of this type have crooked and some have straight legs; and they chase badgers and foxes." Some time later the first printing of Täntzer's *Jagdgeheimnissen* ("Secrets of the Hunt") appeared. Here we find besides "beaverdogs and otterdogs" (*Biber- und Otterhunden*) the mention of a "badgerhound" (*Dachskriecher*) with "especially crooked legs." Accordingly one might believe that the Dachshund was then in existence even though it was not identical to today's dog. The illustration portrays small dogs, which are distantly reminiscent of terriers (*Terrierpinscher*). They are shown as possessing small, stiffly pointed ears and a puglike tail, curled sideways.

The literature of the time also includes such terms as "holedoggie" (*Lochhündlein*), "earthdoggie" (*Erdhündle*), "creeper hound" (*Schliefferlin*), "badger hound" (*Tachsschliefern*), and "dachshund" (*Dachseln*). These names, however, referred to the utilization of these dogs, rather than to a specific breed, a terminology more helpful to the hunter than the dog breeder.

A book published in 1700, Holberg's *Georgica Curiosa*, provides some of the first reliable information about the ancestors of our modern Dachshund. In the section on "Badger-, Otter-, and Beaverdogs" (*Dachsen-, Otter- und Biberhunden*), Holberg states, "These three varieties have about the same hunting accomplishments, but the first variety is especially suited to go after badgers. The French call these particular dogs Bassets (*Bassets*), because of their low structure, their long slender body and their low, somewhat turned in little legs . . ., they have various colors, but mostly brown, gray and otter-colored, sometimes also black." In 1716 the book *Neue lustige und vollständige Jagdkunst* ("New Merry and Complete Huntmanship") was published. It contained the following, "The badger is being hunted with little hounds. . . . As soon as the fox smells these little dogs he sneaks out of the den, with the exception of a vixen with cubs. Nevertheless foxes can sometimes be surprised and caught inside the den by keen little hounds."

Tachs Kriecher, from "Der vollkommene teutsche Jager" by Flemming.

Tachs Krieger, from "Der vollkommene teutsche Jager" by Flemming.

Tachs-Schlieffer, Tachs-Würger, etching by Ridinger.

In 1719 von Flemming published his book *Der vollkommene teutsche Jäger* ("The Complete German Hunter") in which he showed pictures of "Tachs Kriecher" and "Tachs Krieger." These two dogs are, without doubt, the equivalent of our modern Dachshund. Von Flemming wrote that these dogs "trail and chase and track their game, give tongue and point with such diligence and zeal, as any of the others would, to show to the hunter where the game is hidden. This miniature type is most often red or black with dropped ears, practically similar to the Pointer (*Jagdhund*), only smaller like miniatures. . . . To make the young dogs more eager he gets encouragement with cheerful words and blood to get the taste. These Dachshunds are also often used by some people as tracking dogs to search out rabbits and foxes, or to locate weasels and other destructive animals and to exterminate them."

In 1734 von Pärson mentions "small, shortlegged, compact and very snappy dogs, which enjoy entering underground passages."

The famous print of Ridinger also dates from around this time. It shows "Tachs-Schlieffer, Tachs-Würger," which much resembles our Dachshunds.

Dachshund with
straight legs,
by Buffon.

In 1751 von Happe remarks that some Dachshunds are high and others are low to the ground and that some have straight and others have crooked legs like those of the hounds (*Leithunde*). In the book *Jägerpraktika* ("Hunting Practice") Döbel in 1786 demands keen Dachshunds for fox and badger hunting: "It happens that if the dogs are not really keen, the badger sits in a chamber in his den and waits until he is discovered. Then he moves away and rests at a different place; in this way all the initial effort has been in vain."

Buffon in his *Histoire Naturelle* ("Natural History") published in 1793, mentions the crooked-legged and straight-legged Dachshunds; he describes their color as black, fawn, white, or dappled. He reports that Dachshunds are very snappy and chase badgers out of holes. The illustrations by Buffon show that the crooked-legged Dachshunds, even then, tended to knuckle over more than the straight-legged ones. They also showed that the Dachshunds were built low, but not at all in an exaggerated way, had rather long bodies, and were somewhat overdeveloped, like most hunting dogs of those days.

Jester, in 1797, wrote: "The Dachshund is of all the hunting dogs the smallest and the weakest, but he surpasses them all in courage. He searches

Dachshund with
crooked legs,
by Buffon.

for his far superior enemy deep inside the earth and fights him in his own home territory for endless hours, yes, even for days. . . . The uneven dappled and the stockhaired Dachshunds are less common than the black and brown." By "brown" Jester probably meant the color we call "red" today.

In 1812 Dr. Walther said of Dachshunds: "They are snappy, often pugnacious, brave, but often quarrelsome animals, who are tenacious of life. They tend to start fights with any dog, no matter how large he is."

Dr. Walther also mentioned the wirehaired Dachshund and referred to it as a very good worker which is generally "not as low-legged or crooked as the smooth variety." These are characteristics which are still attributed to the wirehairs, and often rightfully so. Dietrich aus dem Winkell mentioned the longhaired Dachshunds in 1820.

The first one to list all varieties was Dr. Reichenbach, in 1836. This is of special interest because only in more recent times did some varieties receive

Dachshunds, one with stockhair, others smooth, in solid color, dappled and brindled, by Dr. Reichenbach (1836).

a fresh impetus through more knowledgeable dog breeding. In his illustrations we see smooth, longhaired, and wirehaired Dachshunds; their colors are black, fawn, brown, dappled, or brindle; and they are shown with crooked and straight legs.

Then came the destructive revolution followed by the terrible years of the fifties. Interest slackened, but Dachshunds were bred here and there without any uniformity among breeders. Yet this breeding was sufficient enough to act as a springboard for later extensive and purposeful breeding.

The year 1879 was of great importance, since this was when the breed characteristics, essentially as they are today, were first standardized. At that time, however, the standard was not as rigid as it is today. The first German studbook contained 54 entries; among these were names of owners who, in the opinion of experts, enjoyed an especially high reputation. Among these were: G. Barnewitz, W. v. Daacke, and Baron v. Knigge.

The exhibition in Berlin in 1883 was a great event. Von Knigge's Dachshunds received the highest awards of the show and the gold medal of Kaiser William I. The Dachshunds of von Knigge were a major influence on the breed. Their names would appear in most pedigrees of today, if one would or could trace them back far enough.

Almost more important for the entire Dachshund breed, and especially for the red-coated Dachshunds, was the stock bred by von Daacke. Wilhelm v. Daacke, of Osterode in the Harz Mountains, belongs forever among the greatest of Dachshund breeders. Many important red Dachshunds of the past and present carry the strain of his bloodlines. Of course many owners are not aware of this fact, because the pedigrees do not go back that far. Wilhelm v. Daacke's father, A. v. Daacke, started to breed in May 1868.* The von Daacke motto was: "*The Dachshund should be bred as a hunting dog, particularly for the hunt below and above the earth. Therefore the dog should weigh a maximum of about 17½ lbs. (8 Kg.) and the bitch a maximum of app. 15½ lbs. (7 Kg.).*" Old, valuable principles, which were sadly neglected

Two of v. Hohenhorst's Smooth Miniature Dachshunds with the Adler girls. Left, Go-Go Girl-M and Evelyn; Right, Georgie Girl-M and Beverly. Owner Leonore Loeb Adler. Photo by Dr. Helmut E. Adler.

* Mrs. Luise von Daacke pointed out that Dr. Engelmann was in error with the date; it should read May 1861, instead. Chief Forestry Ranger August v. Daacke had kept Dachshunds previously, but started his programmed breeding in 1861. L.L.A.

Ch. Westphal's Timber and Westphal's Berry helping Judy Castoral with her homework. Owner Mary Castoral. Photo by Frank Castoral.

during the following decades when Dachshund breeding became submerged in the general breeding of dogs. At the start, however, von Daacke used heavier Dachshunds, some weighing 19¾ lbs. (9 Kg.). The most famous of them all was "Monsieur Schneidig." In Berlin this dog entered into competition with "Flott-Sonnenberg," who was also a highly meritorious sire, though "Monsieur Schneidig" was somewhat superior to him in the shape of his head. It is said of the von Daacke dogs, that the early heavy breeding stock contained some blood of the best Harzer Bloodhounds. (*Translator's note: In private correspondence, Mr. Wilhelm von Daacke, of Dannenberg a/d Elbe—grandson and son of the Messrs. v. Daacke mentioned above—explained to me that these dogs should not be mistaken for the American or English Bloodhound, but are a smaller type, more like the "Bracke," and very efficient in trailing.*) If the introduction of "Bloodhound" blood actually occurred it would surely not be a disadvantage, considering both the close relationship of the two breeds and that the Dachshund may really be thought of as a "small Bloodhound." Even today there are small "Bloodhounds"; all that is needed is to breed them lower to give them a remarkable likeness to the red smooth Dachshunds. The loose shoulders are also characteristic of both breeds, and desirable at that, since they facilitate mobility and keeping the nose close to the ground. It was often the case that these red Dachshunds had dark masks, which looked very good. It is a pity that today the red Dachshund no longer shows this mask. In former days those dogs with masks were especially selected, as they had the reputation of being the best Dachshunds for work on blood trails.

Whatever "Monsieur Schneidig" and "Flott-Sonnenberg" were to the red Dachshund, "Hundesports Waldmann" and "Schlupfer-Euskirchen" were to the black-and-tan. Both of the latter, as were actually many black-and-tan Dachshunds, were descended from "Dachs" (*T.St.B.*—Dachshund studbook 16); his origin could never be determined, but he exhibited a remarkable prepotency.

DACHSHUNDS IN GERMANY

By Anneliese Wurm

(Member of the D.T.K. and international writer on Dachshund topics.)

"Teckel, Dackel, Dachshund—though these are different names, they refer to the same breed: self confident and reliable and therefore so well liked." (Here paraphrased for clarity.)

The *Deutscher Teckel Klub* (German Teckel Club), the parent club of the Dachshund breed in Germany, chose the above slogan as their public relations motto. While "Dachshund" is the original and official name of the breed, Teckel and Dackel are nothing more than "idiomatic expressions," common terms used frequently in the north and in the south of Germany respectively. The very popular Dachshund is somewhat of a national breed and in the country of its origin* is outranked only by the German Shepherd.

The Dachshund has been chosen as the mascot of the 1972 Olympic Games, in Munich, Germany. As souvenirs of many different types, the "Olympia Dachshund WALDI" will leave the country after the games to advertise the breed all over the world.

In Germany, the breed is represented by the "Deutscher Teckel Klub"

---

* *Although Germany is generally accepted as the Dachshund's origin, I show that it probably can be traced to the Middle Kingdom, ca. 2,000 B.C. in ancient Egypt (see p. 126–133).* *L.L.A.*

Emblem and slogan of the Deutscher Teckelklub.

Leonore Loeb Adler (left) and Anneliese Wurm with two-week-old litter of Vom Fürstenfels puppies. Photo by Dr. Helmut E. Adler.

(D.T.K.), which was founded in 1888. This is where the studbook is kept —the only German Dachshund studbook acknowledged by all kennel clubs in the world. In 1970, the D.T.K. had a membership of 15,209. Many of these members, owners of just one or sometimes more Dachshunds, are interested in learning more about the breed. Though many do not intend to breed in the beginning, eventually, they get so involved, that they become enthusiastic breeders of Dachshunds.

Besides the standard on conformation and points for evaluation, the D.T.K. has introduced rules for breeding and field trials. The aim of the D.T.K. is to breed a Dachshund, equally as perfect in conformation to the standard (beauty), as in work in the field. (Never forget that Dachshunds belong to the hound group, being a hunting breed.) Dachshunds are bred in three coat varieties: Smooth; Wire and Longhair; and in three sizes: Standard (app. 6 to 9 kg., or 14 to 19 lbs.), Miniature, and Rabbit. Since many hunters wanted a very small dog to chase after rabbits and to replace the ferret, the Rabbit Dachshund came into existence in the beginning of this century and was created solely for this purpose and by no means for reasons of the fancy. Although the Standard Dachshund was bred down to Miniature

Dachshund *(Zwergteckel)* and then to Rabbit Dachshund *(Kaninchenteckel)*, breeders could never forget that these were still hounds. In both of these smaller size varieties, the Dachshund is classified according to its chest circumference which is no more than 13¾ inches (35 *centimeters*) for Miniature Dachshunds, and 11¾ inches (30 *centimeters*) for Rabbit Dachshunds. This measurement is snugly taken around the highest point of the withers and the lowest part of the thorax. As long as the Dachshund is within the limits of these measurements and at least fifteen months old, he should be looked over by a judge to confirm these facts. Only then can the pedigree be completed by listing a *Zw* (for *Zwerg* or Miniature) or *Kt* (for *Kaninchenteckel*, Rabbit Dachshund) in the studbook afterwards becoming a part of the registration number.

Some of the breeding rules enforced by the D.T.K. protecting bitches and dogs from exploitation are concerned with maintaining the high quality of the Dachshunds.

Vom Fürstenfels' Perle and Pankraz; breeder-owner of Miniature and Rabbit Dachshunds Anneliese Wurm. Photo by Anneliese Wurm.

BREEDING RULES

Neither dam nor sire is allowed to be bred under one year of age. A certified judge has to give each a rating, which in case of the dog (sire) has to be at least "Very Good," and "Good" for the bitch (dam). When a dog is judged "Good," he is acceptable for breeding only if he is outstanding in field trial work. The three highest ratings are "Excellent" *(Vorzüglich)*, "Very Good" *(Sehr Gut)* and "Good" *(Gut)*.

Two successive heats can be used for breeding only if spaced nine months or more apart.

When the puppies are between eight to ten weeks old, the litters have to be inspected and tattooed by a "Breeding Inspector" *(Zuchtwart des D.T.K.)*, before they can be registered in the studbook. Puppies with serious faults, such as overshot or undershot jaws, crooked tail or "chicken breast," to name a few, receive the notation on their pedigree of "Not to be used for breeding purposes."

Crossing of coat varieties is not at all permitted. In 1970 the D.T.K. studbook recorded a total of 18,322 puppies (all coats). Listed separately by

Two of Schuco's "Olympia Dachshund Waldi" being loved and hugged by Elizabeth A. Kahn of Long Island, N.Y. Photo by Dr. Helmut E. Adler.

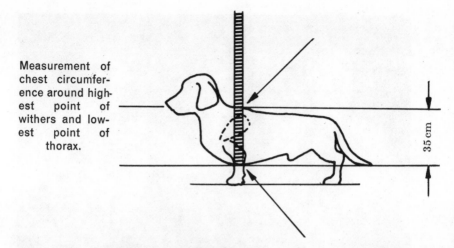

Measurement of chest circumference around highest point of withers and lowest point of thorax.

35 cm

coat varieties there were 813 Smooths, 7,906 Wires, and 9,603 Longs. When comparing these figures with those of former years, it becomes obvious that the number of Smooths is decreasing continuously. For instance in 1959 a total of 14,080 puppies (all coats) was recorded in the

Laurin vom Fürstenfels, a dappled Miniature Dachshund; breeder-owner Anneliese Wurm. Photo by same.

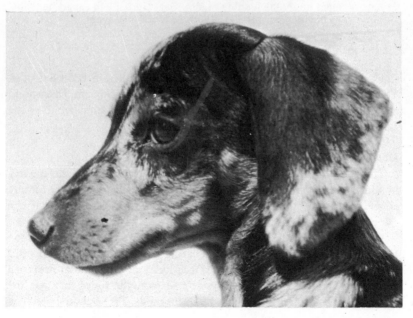

Batzenhof's Ch. Chiko vom Pagenhof, CACIB and CAC, was imported from Germany by his co-owners Kurt and Irma Mickley of Louisiana. Here he is Best of Winners under the judging of Mrs. Gary Gerber and expert handling of Hannelore Heller. Photo by Marion Seavers.

studbook, which when divided by coat varieties resulted in 1,359 Smooths, 3,820 Wires, and 8,901 Longs. Since the war the Smooth Dachshund appears to be no longer "in fashion," and is readily outnumbered by the Longhair Dachshund.

DOG SHOWS

There are different types of "shows" held in every part of the country in which Dachshunds can be judged on conformation *(Formwert)* scoring either "Excellent," "Very Good," or "Good" then determining if the Dachshund can qualify for breeding purposes.

The general "Breed Show" *(Zuchtschau)* run by a regional group of the D.T.K. is very popular. Instead of having classes and competition this show acts as a gathering place for Dachshund people of local areas. In explaining his decision to the ringside audience, the judge instructs the newcomers about merits and faults in Dachshunds. Two hundred and nine such Breed Shows were held in 1970 with a total entry of 6,837 Dachshunds of at least nine months of age.

There are several kinds of "Open Shows" which are sponsored either by Breed Clubs and/or by the V.d.H. *(Verband für das deutsche Hundewesen)*, which is the German Kennel Club. Having competitions in different classes, these shows present opportunities to win special titles. For example, the individual German States, such as Bavaria, Hesse, Baden, Württemberg, put on an annual Regional Championship Show *(Landessiegerschau)* which offers the title of Regional Champion *(Landessieger)* for a specific State.

In the annual National Championship Show *(Bundessiegerschau)* including all of the German States, the title of National Champion *(Bundessieger)* can be won. Some of the shows are CC shows, where the CACIB *(Certicates d'Aptitude au Championat Internationale de Beauté)* is offered by the F.C.I. *(Fédération International Cinologique)*, which is the International Kynological Federation, the head organization of the participating kennel clubs in Europe. In all of these shows, Dachshunds are entered in different classes separated by the three coat varieties, by the three sizes and by the two sexes, and the CACIB is offered to each top winner in each category. Eighteen CACIB's can be won by the entries after fulfilling the following conditions for Top Rating: Excellent, and for the Age—at least 15 months old. If none of the entries in a category are good enough to receive an "Excellent," then the CACIB is withheld. In 1970 there were twenty of these Regional Championship and International Championship Shows with an entry of 1,872.

The International Championship for Beauty can be earned by a Dachshund who has won two CACIB's in two different countries, under two different judges, at least one year apart, and in addition must have received a field trial certificate, either a BhFK or a BhFN for successful work with a live fox under the earth, in an artificial den or in a natural burrow respectively. These conditions are the same for all size varieties. (A dog may earn several CACIB's during one year, but these do not count toward the International Championship title.)

FIELD TRIALS

Field trials are held in order to judge and promote the hunting ability and performance of the Dachshund. The most important breed characteristics are: work under the earth, trailing and flushing, following the scent, giving tongue, sharpness in tracking, and staying steadily on the trail.

Field trial certificates can be earned in the following areas:

1. Aptitude for work in the den (artificial and/or natural dens).
2. Giving tongue.
3. Tracking trial (on artificial or natural trail).

4. Flushing and trailing.

5. Versatility trial (combinations of accomplishments).

6. Rabbit drag (for Rabbit Dachshunds) and trial in natural warren with live rabbit.

In 1970, a total of 333 Field Trials were held with an entry of 3,327 Dachshunds of which 2,271 passed the tests successfully thereby receiving their well-earned certificates.

The D.T.K. also keeps a special "Working Dachshund Studbook" for Field Trial work. All Dachshunds, who have passed a den aptitude trial in an artificial or a natural den and who have proved that they can give tongue or who have passed both trials within a versatility trial, are registered in this studbook.

In 1970, the Working Dachshund Studbook registered 238 Dachshunds fulfilling the condition specified above.

50 YEARS OF DACHSHUNDS
IN THE BRITISH ISLES

By Angel Negal

(President of the Miniature Dachshund Club, Chairman of the Eastern Counties Dachshund Association, and Hon. Secretary of the Dachshund Council.)

INTRODUCTION

Since the competitive spirit has always been strong in me when I felt I could no longer continue a fairly successful hobby in car trials, I found myself drawn into the complexities of dog breeding and showing during the late 1930's. When I entered the R.A.F. in 1941, I was a reasonably successful exhibitor of Wirehaired Fox Terriers and Smoothhaired and Miniature Smoothhaired Dachshunds. I then had the best Miniature smooth bitch at Crufts 1939 and the best Miniature smooth dog and bitch at Richmond Championship Show in the same year, therefore, I had "seeing knowledge" of Dachshunds prior to World War II. During the war years, my kennel virtually disappeared and I returned to find one remaining dog which I could use. I bought Ch. Zeus von Schwarenberg's granddaughter from Mme. Rikovsky, which I mated to this dog and thus founded the post-war Montreux Kennel. They have since produced for me thirty-two homebred English champions in addition to the one from Mme. Rikovsky.

Ch. Rhinefields Diplomat; co-owners Mr. and Mrs. John Gallup.

SMOOTHHAIRED DACHSHUNDS

After World War I, Major Hayward was the only Dachshund enthusiast who had been able to keep a kennel supreme in both breeding and exhibition stock. This was, of course, the famous "Honey" strain. In 1923 Mr. Dunlop imported Theo von Neumarkt and his son Ch. Remagen Max who was to have a great effect on the English Dachshund. Max sired eight champions; the most important being Ch. Honeytime, the sire of five champions. In 1924 Mr. Dunlop imported Ch. Faust von Faustenberg, whose combination with the daughters of Max was a further step in the improvement of the breed. In 1922 Mrs. Huggins bought an imported dog, Friedel von Taunerbrund, and mated him to English-bred bitches of the "Honey" strain, creating the famous "Firs" strain.

The "Firs" success was heightened after Mme. Rikovsky's importation of Ch. Wolf von Birkenschloss, who sired four "Firs" champions. Ch. Zwieback von der Howitt, the son of Wolf, was the sire of another four "Firs" champions, including the famous Ch. Firs Black Velvet. In 1926 Mme. Rikovsky bought the bitch Isolde von Faustenberg, that when mated to Ch. Remagen Max produced her foundation stock. Mme. Rikovsky's importance grew as the result of her selection and importation of young dogs, but especially (to me) after the importation of Ch. Zeus von

41

Schwarenberg, for he not only sired a number of smoothhaired champions, but also carried longhaired recessive genes.

Major Hayward ceased to exhibit in 1923 and the cream of his kennel was purchased by Colonel Spurrier for his daughter, Miss Spurrier of "Querns" fame. Miss Spurrier further strengthened the "Querns" when on the death of Mr. Dunlop she purchased Ch. Faust von Faustenberg and Theo von Neumarkt.

Mrs. Grosvenor-Workman's "Silvae" prefix was registered in 1935, and after World War II when exhibiting recommenced, it became the outstanding kennel. The great winner at that time was Ch. Silvae Lustre, sired by Ch. Silvae Zebo. The importance of Ch. Zeus is now clear, he was the sire of Ch. Zebo. Zebo himself was the sire of nine champions, but as a sire was completely overshadowed by his grandson Ch. Silvae Sailors Quest, the result of mating a son of Zebo, Ch. Silvae Banjo, to a Zebo daughter, Ch. Silvae Polish.

Quest had only a short life of five years, but during this period sired twenty-one English champions including three litters with three champions in each. His best son was Ch. Ashdown Skipper, the sire of six champions. It was strange that although Quest sired this host of champions, he did not produce a champion for his owner. When this fact was mentioned to Miss Workman, she replied that the demands for his services as a sire were so great that there was little opportunity to use him for their own stock. Quest's sire, Ch. Silvae Banjo, was also the sire of Ch. Silvae Bandoleer who, like Quest, was also the result of mating a son of Zebo to a Zebo daughter, Ch. Silvae Land Girl. Bandoleer was the sire of eight champions.

After the untimely death of Quest, the line was carried strongly through his sons, Ch. Ashdown Skipper, and Turlshill Pirate, owned by Mr. Pinches, as well as Quest's half-brother, Ch. Silvae Bandoleer. Turlshill Pirate was used extensively by the breeders in the '60s and has had much to do with present day winning stock.

In addition, many world-famous kennels emerged in this era: the "Aysdorn" of Mr. and Mrs. Crowley; the "Selwood" of Mrs. Hood-Wright; the "Hawkstone" of Miss Hill; the "Kelvindale" of Mrs. Collins and others. Mr. A. W. Hague's "Limberin" prefix, founded in 1935, was strengthened by his use of Ch. Zeus von Schwarenberg producing his first champion, Ch. Limberin Lounge Lizard in the early '50s. Through careful breeding and buying, back on the Ch. Silvae Bandoleer and Ch. Ashdown Skipper line, Hague produced Ch. Limberin Timaru Thunderbolt and Ch. Limberin Lore Lei, and through Ch. Hawkstone Fusilier, Ch. L. Leading Light. By mating Leading Light to Lore Lei, he produced Ch. L. Lamp Lighter who sired Ch. L. Leading Lady, one of the outstanding bitches of 1969. The "Silvae" kennel continued to produce champions by mating back on the Ch. Silvae Bandoleer line, two of the latest being Ch. S. Kerris and Ch. S. Frere, grandchildren of Bandoleer. This line will produce many more up and coming champions in the ring today.

The "Womack" kennel of Mr. and Mrs. Gale produced the famous Ch. Womack Wrightstarturn . . . winner of thirty-eight challenge certificates, including three times Best of Breed at Crufts—who became a force in the showring in the early '60s. Womack Wagonette, a descendant of Quest's son Ch. Urbaz von der Howitt, was mated to Turlshill Pirate producing Ch. Womack Wainwright. Wainwright was the sire of Wrightstarturn and eight other champions. Their present day champion and winning stock are based on blood lines dating back to Zeus through Pirate and latterly through Ch. Rhinefields Diplomat, the sire of Ch. Womack Wrazzamatazz. The "Rhine-fields" kennel of Mr. and Mrs. Gallop was based on a daughter of Ch. Zeus, mated to a Quest's son, Ch. Urbaz von der Howitt. With line breeding to Turlshill Pirate and careful inbreeding on the resultant stock, they have been able to produce such notable champions as Ch. Rhinefields Diplomat, which won the Dachshund Club's "Jackdaw" Trophy for the greatest winner of all coats in 1968, and his litter sister, Ch. Rhinefields Dolabella, the leading bitch of the breed in 1968 and 1969.

LONGHAIRED DACHSHUNDS

The importation of Ratzmann vom Habichthof in 1922 by Mrs. Quicke seemed to be the foundation of the longhaired Dachshund in this Country. His debut in the showring at Crufts in 1923 against Major Hayward's smoothhaired won him the challenge certificate. A great deal of inbreeding took place to keep this breed alive with only a limited number of bitches.

When the longhaired breed was granted challenge certificates in 1931, Lieutenant Colonel Bedford imported Elfe von Fels in whelp to Stropp von der Winberg resulting in Ch. Rufus of Armadale and Ch. Rose of Armadale. During 1931, every challenge certificate winner carried Lieutenant Colonel Bedford's prefix, and although they were not all owned by him, they had all been bred by him. That same year Mrs. Bellamy bought Ch. Chloe of Armadale, and Mrs. Reade bought Ch. Captain of Armadale from Lieutenant Colonel Bedford who then decided that more imported blood was needed and consequently imported Otter von Fels. This dog also became a champion.

During this period, both line breeding and inbreeding took place. Mrs. Bellamy mated Ch. Rufus of Armadale to Ch. Chloe of Armadale, both offspring of Elfe von Fels, the result being Ch. Michael von Walder. In 1934 Mrs. Bellamy took Drusilla of Armadale (daughter of Ch. Rufus of Armadale, son of Ch. Rose of Armadale, this being brother and sister mating) to Ch. Otter von Fels. The result of this mating produced Ch. Karl von Walder and Ch. Micheline von Walder. This line and inbreeding by both Lieutenant Colonel Bedford and Mrs. Bellamy had a great influence on the early success of the longhaired Dachshunds.

In 1931 Mrs. Smith-Rewse bought her foundation bitch, Bluebell of Armadale, from Lieutenant Colonel Bedford. Bluebell was then mated to Ch. Rufus of Armadale and the result was Ch. Golden Patch. Lieutenant Colonel Bedford had no further success in the showring although success was achieved by those who bought or used his stock.

In the '40s the "von Walder" prefix, the "Hilltrees" prefix of Lieutenant Colonel Hodge, the "Brincliffe" prefix of Miss K. Cheavey, the "von Holzner" prefix of Mrs. Connel, the "Royce" prefix of Mrs. Joyce and the "Buckmead" prefix of Mrs. Buck and others had success in the ring. It was in the early '50s that a new bloodline was introduced into the longhaired Dachshunds. The longhaired Imber Black Coffee—bred by Miss Raine—was produced, this being the result of a mating of two smooths, which carried the recessive longhaired blood of the smooth dog, Ch. Zeus von Schwarenberg. Imber Black Coffee was mated to a longhaired and produced Ch. Imber Coffee Bean, who was to have a tremendous influence on the

Ch. Red Rheingold of Albany; owner Mrs. K. Jenson. Photo by Diane Pearce.

44

breed. He was the sire of twelve champions, the best being Dr. Raven's Ch. Kennhaven Caesar, winner of over forty challenge certificates and sire of a number of champions.

The recessive longhaired blood of Ch. Zeus von Schwarenberg again manifested itself in Ch. Zoe Celeste of Albany when Mrs. Jensen mated two smooth descendants of Ch. Zeus. The influence of Ch. Imber Coffee Bean was such that practically every longhaired champion carried his name in its pedigree. The result of these two longhaireds was the establishment of the "Albany" prefix. Almost dominating the longhaired Dachshunds in the showring, the Albany line included such notables as the outstanding bitch, Ch. Rebecca of Albany—winning her thirtieth challenge certificate at eight-and-a-half years of age—and the latest successful champion, Ch. Red Rheingold of Albany.

In the longhaireds, the only kennel not to contain the Zeus blood is the "Buckmead" of Mrs. Buck. This strain has been used to advantage in balancing the Zeus blood. The "Buckmead" prefix, which has helped in this way, includes Ch. Buckmead Palomino and his sons Ch. Buckmead Dominic and Ch. Buckmead Hermes.

WIREHAIRED DACHSHUNDS

Wirehaired Dachshunds became of note in England in 1927, when Mr. Fisher imported a number of wires. These included Fritzl von Paulinenberg and Brita of Tavistone in whelp to Wicht St. Georg. When Mr. Rattee bought Fritzl and Brita, they were made champions. Brita, born of Rex von Oetting ex Kathe von Keltergarton, was grey and brown. One of the puppies produced by this pre-import mating of Brita was Flott of Tavistone. Mrs. Blandy's imported bitch, Anna of Nunneshall, was mated to Flott, producing Ch. Achsel and Ch. Anneta. Fritzl was also very successful as a sire, and when mated to Mrs. Blandy's Anneta, produced Ch. Astra; to Mrs. Howard's Flapper of Seale produced Ch. Friedl of Seale; and to Mrs. Allen's Ferwood Walda produced Ch. Einschen of Inverfan. When a breed was imported it became the usual practice to line and inbreed with these importations, usually with good results. It was so with the wires and a considerable amount took place to establish type.

On Mr. Rattee's death in 1931, Mrs. Howard and Lady Schuster in partnership acquired Flott of Tavistone and his daughter Ch. Diana of Tavistone, and also Brownie of Seale, a daughter of Fritzl and Brita, which strengthened the Seale Kennel. The two outstanding stud dogs of the time were Flott of Tavistone and his son, Ch. Achsel. Ch. Achsel was bred by Mrs. Blandy and bought by Miss Theo Watts. Siring six champions, he proved to be the outstanding stud dog of the English-born sires.

In 1934 Air Vice-Marshal Sir Charles Lambe, Miss Theo Watts, Mrs.

Ch. Gisbourne Inca; owner Mrs. B. Farrand. Photo by Ann Roslin-Williams.

MacCaw and Mr. S. Joel formed a syndicate to import Sports Mentor II from Sweden. Mentor was the sire of Ch. Helen of Dunkerque which became the property of Miss Watts, and of Ch. Hero of Dunkerque, which subsequently went to the U.S.A. Sports Mentor II will be seen later to have had an influence on the wirehaired Dachshunds through the Wylde Kennel. Miss Seton-Buckley imported from Sweden in 1937 Wizden Sports Primavera by Spielmann von St. Georg ex Sports Gruffa in whelp to Sports Troll. Primavera became an international champion.

At the end of World War II, the main wirehaired kennels were the "Seale" of Mrs. Howard, the "Seton" of Miss Seton-Buckley and the "Wylde" of Miss Evans. The Seale Kennel was based on the Fritzl, Flott and Brita lines, the Seton Kennel on the Primavera and the Wylde Kennel on a mating of Trix of Dunkerque, a daughter of Sports Mentor II, to a smooth, Wylde Rory. Wylde Rory was by the smooth champion Firs Black Sheen, a grandson of Mme. Rikovsky's smooth importation, Ch. Wolf von Birkenschloss. This latter mating produced Ch. Wylde Encore and Ch. Wylde Enchanter. The result of the pre-import mating of Ch. Primavera had produced for the Seton Kennels a dog called Petroucka of Seton who sired Irish Ch.

Paganini of Seton which in turn sired English Ch. Midas of Seton and his brother, Mercury. Miss Evans took Ch. Wylde Enchanter to Midas of Seton thus producing four champions and then to Mercury producing two champions. Using Midas and Mercury, the Wylde Kennel had eight champions. All Miss Evans' champions seem to have been bred in the space of four years after which her active breeding of the wirehaired Dachshunds seemed to have ended. The continuing importance of the Seton strain can be seen by its offspring. Ch. Midas, mated to a bitch from Mr. J. Lloyd's "Grunwald" strain, produced Ch. Georg of Wytchend and Ch. Gerhardt of Wytchend for Major and Mrs. Ellis-Hughes. Ch. Gerhardt was the sire of Mr. J. Lloyd's Int. Ch. Grunwald Graduate, later purchased by Mr. Farrand.

Several kennels became noteworthy in the 1950's. The "Cloud" Kennel of Mrs. MacCaw received strength from the import of a dog called Hobel aus dem Lohegau. This dog, mated to the smooth bitch, Querns Silhouette, produced Ch. Altair of the Clouds. Dr. Rigg of the "Simonswood" prefix mated a wire bitch, Simonswood Cherry, to the smooth Ch. Allways Popcorn of Thistleavon, who was the son of Ch. Silvae Sailors Quest. The result of this mating was three wire champions, one of which—Sabina—was mated to Ch. Altair of the Clouds, and produced a further three champions. Mrs. Howard's Seale Kennel improved tremendously by outcrossing judiciously when necessary; one notable was Honey Bun of Seale, the dam of three champions. Mrs. Farrand, owner of the record-breaking dog Ch. Gisbourne Inca, bred by Mrs. Quick, is the foremost exhibitor of wirehaired Dachshunds today. His picture, showing his normal stance, will give some idea of his superior quality. Inca's dam, Gisbourne Camilla, was line bred to Int. Ch. Grunwald Graduate who appears three times as the grandsire. Mrs. Farrand is not only an outstanding exhibitor of today but she has also bred and owned many outstanding champions in the past twenty years.

Some others who are strong in the breed today are: Mrs. Hoxey-Harris with the "Tumlow" strain; Miss Raine with the "Imber"; Dr. Blair with the "Tentsmuir"; Miss Hughes with the "Meeching" and Miss Raphael with the "Andyce".

SMOOTHHAIRED MINIATURE DACHSHUNDS

Between the two world wars, smoothhaired Miniature Dachshunds were struggling to establish themselves as a separate breed. Among the pioneers in this venture were the Bletchingham Kennel of Mrs. Whiteley, the Seale Kennel of Mrs. Howard and the Taschen Kennel of Dr. Blakiston and Miss New. They all relied greatly on importations from abroad. My own "Montreux" prefix, registered in 1936, commenced when I bought a

Ch. Prince Albert of Wendlitt (winner of the Challenge Certificate of Crufts in 1968, 1969, 1970 and 1971); owner Mrs. Littmoden. Photo by Thomas Fall.

litter out of a longhaired bitch, Zwerg Teeflette, bred by Major Reynall and mated to an imported longhaired dog of Mrs. Howard, Maiklang aus dem Lohegau of Seale. In this litter was a smooth red Miniature dog, Mauritania of Montreux. I mated this dog to a tiny Standard bitch, Angels Serenade of Montreux, which I bought from Mr. Ricks, and thus produced Black Watch of Montreux, the foundation of my strain. After World War II, Mrs. Whiteley ceased breeding, and the remaining strains had a great struggle. Since Black Watch, then eight years old, was my only remaining dog, I bought a tiny chocolate Standard granddaughter of Ch. Zeus von Schwarenberg from Mme. Rikovsky. This was Contessina of Montreux, Best Miniature all Coats for 1947–1948, who became the first smooth Miniature bitch champion in 1949 when challenge certificates were first allocated—a charming, gallant little lady. I then mated Contessina to Black Watch, and their litter produced a dog, Prince John of Montreux, and a bitch, Titania of Montreux, from which I founded my post-war strain.

At this time Mrs. Winder's famous Minivale Kennel came to the fore. She had purchased a bitch, Nettle Danger, which descended on one side from Mrs. Whiteley's Bletchingham strain and on the other from Standard stock. Mating her into the Taschen strain produced a grandson, Minivale Majestic, who produced four champions and founded some famous strains. Majestic was mated to a tiny Standard bitch and produced the first smooth Miniature champion dog, Ch. Minivale Miraculous. Miraculous was mated to his sister, and this mating produced the famous smooth Miniature dog, Ch. Minivale Melvin, and his sisters, Ch. Minivale Miranda and Ch. Minivale Marta of Sillwood, bought by Mrs. Wakefield. Melvin had a tremendous influence on the breed, for he sired eight champions, and no major winning strain is without his blood. Through line and inbreeding on this stock Mrs. Winder continued very successfully for some years, but this was her zenith.

Mr. and Mrs. Fox of Shepherdsdene took a daughter of Trinket of Bletchingham, Glare of Shepherdsdene, to Minivale Majestic and produced Ch. Shepherdsdene Sensation. Subsequently, through careful breeding on this strain, plus the occasional introduction of outside blood by bitch lines, the Shepherdsdene have continued to produce winning show stock, noted for clear reds and fawns with dark points, their latest champion being Ch. Shepherdsdene Rhine Wine.

From Mrs. Winder, Mrs. Littmoden bought a daughter produced by Majestic and a small Standard bitch, and made her into the famous champion, Minivale Matinnee Girl, the base of the Wendlitt Kennel today. Majestic's son, Ch. Minivale Miraculous, was the sire of eight champions. Mrs. Bassett took a bitch of the existing blood lines to Miraculous and produced Ch. Merryweather Matilda. Mrs. Littmoden and Mrs. Bassett mated back these two foundation bitches, Ch. Minivale Matinnee Girl and Ch. Merryweather Matilda, to Miraculous's son, Ch. Minivale Melvin, and the resulting litters were most important to the continuation of their strains. Mrs. Littmoden produced three champions from the Melvin ex Matinnee Girl mating—Ch. Otter of Wendlitt, Ch. Gaiety of Wendlitt and later Ch. Career Girl of Wendlitt. Ch. Otter of Wendlitt sired four champions, among them my own Ch. Courtney of Montreux, and Mr. and Mrs. Newbury's Ch. Dalegarth Tielwood Sally, the first champion of the successful Dalegarth Kennels. His last champion was Ch. Septimus of Wendlitt, result of Otter's mating to a daughter of Ch. Merryweather Murgatroyd.

The most outstanding dog in the showring today is Mrs. Littmoden's Ch. Prince Albert of Wendlitt, winner of the challenge certificate of Crufts from 1968 to 1971, holding the record for the most challenge certificates won by any smooth Miniature. His sire, Ch. Dandy Dan of Wendlitt—a grandson of Ch. Otter of Wendlitt, Ch. Minivale Matinnee Girl, Ch. Minivale Melvin and my own Ch. Stephan of Montreux—and his dam, Ch. Wendlitt Tessa of Hobbithill, were bred by Dr. Kershaw from lines going back to Minivale and Merryweather strains.

The result of Mrs. Bassett's mating of Ch. Merryweather Matilda to Ch. Minivale Melvin were the two dogs, Ch. Merryweather Magic and Ch. Merryweather Marvel. Producing eleven champions, Magic was the greatest smooth Miniature sire. Marvel was the sire of five, and, through his son Ch. Merryweather Matthew, was the grandsire of Ch. Merryweather Murgatroyd, one of the best dogs to be shown. Mrs. Bassett's Merryweather Kennel is still forceful with champion Merryweather Masquerade and his progeny, Ch. Merryweather Maddalo Sweet Honey, bred by Miss Glover, and Mrs. Evans and Mrs. Angus's Ch. Amberleigh Red Rufus of Gilston, bred by Mrs. Marshall.

I mated Prince John of Montreux back to his dam, Ch. Contessina, and produced Ch. Stephan of Montreux, winner of fourteen challenge certificates. In his short life of three years he was widely used and influenced other strains to some degree. I mated Prince John to the cream of my Standard bitches and selected the best to mate back to Stephan, thereby producing several champions. Feeling the need to outcross, I then mated Ch. Mariella of Montreux, the first under-nine-pound champion, to Mrs. Bassett's Ch. Merryweather Marvel. The litter produced a dog, Cassandra, and two bitches, Cressida and Helen. Cassandra's mating to Prince John's litter sister, Titania, produced Ch. Romulus of Montreux, the sire of seven champions, including Mrs. Blandford's champion, Ch. Flaunden Senator. By mating Romulus back to his sire's sister, Cressida, I bred Ch. Shulamede that has had a great influence on my stock, and Ch. Magdaleine. From mating Romulus back to his sire's other sister Helen, I bred Ch. Bartolo and

Ch. Cedric, and also my second under-nine-pound champion, Ch. Carmenita, who weighed seven-and-a-quarter pounds.

I next took Cressida to Mrs. Littmoden's Ch. Otter of Wendlitt, which produced Ch. Courtney and his sister, Carol. Carol is at sixteen a fine old lady, and her progeny have been of great value, especially her daughter Magnolia, the dam of five champions. Romulus, when mated to a granddaughter of the brother and sister mating of Prince John and Titania, produced for me Ch. Chocoletta, which I took to Mrs. Bassett's Ch. Merryweather Murgatroyd. The resulting litter gave me Ramiro of Montreux, who sired seven champions including Ch. Geoffrey and Ch. Cavalier. After buying a smooth Miniature silver dapple bitch from Miss Raine's Imber kennel and taking her to Ch. Romulus, the daughter produced was mated with Ramiro's chocolate son, Ch. Cavalier, producing the only English smooth Miniature champion, Ch. Bellini. He is now owned by Mme. Galliene in France, where he is an International Champion. By line breeding and inbreeding my very large kennel, I have bred thirty-two Miniature champions, the latest being Ch. Irving of Montreux, Ch. Soraya and Ch. Arturus.

There are now many notable kennels in existence that have developed from the basic post-war lines of the "Minivale," "Wendlitt," "Merryweather," "Montreux" and "Shepherdsdene." Among them is Mr. A. W. Hague's "Limberin" kennel, based on a mixture of small Standards with "Minivale" and "Merryweather" lines. Ch. Limberin Americano, the sire of four champions, and the latest, Ch. Limberin Pan Americano are two of his best. Other successful kennels are: Dr. Kershaw's Hobbithill strain, breeder of five champions, Mrs. Blandford's Flaunden Kennel, Mr. and Mrs. Smith's Wimoway Kennel, Flight Lieutenant Pugh's Tarkotta Kennel, Mrs. Samuel's Bettmark Kennel, Miss Barker's Potsdown Kennel, Mrs. Foden's Booth Kennel and the outstanding Bowbank Kennel of Mr. and Mrs. Solomon which produced that great champion, Ch. Bowbank Red Riordan, winner of thirty-four challenge certificates.

LONGHAIRED MINIATURE DACHSHUNDS

The interest in the Miniature longs began in the early 1930's and at first they forged ahead of the smooth Miniatures. A number were imported by Miss Dixon and Major Reynall, the most notable being Holodri von Fleezensee who when mated to an imported bitch of Miss Herdman, sired Knowlton Chocolate Soldier. Mrs. Smith-Rewse's developing interest in Miniature longs led her to mate Zwerg Golden Primrose to Knowlton Chocolate Soldier, so producing Goldlein and Roselein of Primrosepatch. Goldlein and Roselein were the dams of Meadow Sweet of Primrosepatch, and of Black Watch of Primrosepatch respectively. When viewing the

51

pedigree of Mrs. Portman-Graham's Ch. Marcus of Mornyvarna, the first Miniature champion, it will be seen that his sire Otta of Mornyvarna was out of Meadow Sweet of Primrosepatch, and his dam Mitzi of Mornyvarna was sired by Black Watch of Primrosepatch. Marcus himself was the sire of eight champions and had a great influence on Miniature longs in general. Another notable sire, Mrs. Ireland-Blackburne's Ch. Robsvarl Red Robin, has a pedigree going back—like Marcus's—to Goldlein of Primrosepatch, Holodri von Fleezensee and Knowlton Chocolate Soldier.

The first Miniature long was Ch. Chloe von Walder bred by Mrs. Bellamy, and sired by Ch. Robsvarl Red Robin ex Minnette von Walder a bitch of the Knowlton Chocolate Soldier line. In 1950, Mrs. Gwyer of the "Marlenwood" prefix, breeding to Primrosepatch and Red Robin line, bred Ch. Jamie of Marlenwood and Ch. Priorsgate Marlenwood Royce. The outstanding sire, Royce, bought by Miss Sherer, became the sire of five champions, including Ch. Springmount Madrigal bred by Mrs. Marsh.

It was around this time that a certain amount of smooth Miniature blood was incorporated into the Miniature longs. Ch. John of Mornyvarna, son of Marcus, sired the Miniature smooth, Ch. Querns Tango of Gladsmuir, out of the Miniature smooth Ch. Tallullah of Gladsmuir. Tango was mated to the Miniature smooth bitch Tosdig Ferda, and produced Ch. Fricasse of Mallards, a Miniature long—this was Mrs. S. Gale's first champion. Fricasse was mated to Ch. Springmount Madrigal and produced Ch. Don Basilio of Mallards and Madrilene of Mallards. Madrilene was mated to the smooth Miniature Merryweather Mahogany, who carried the Primrosepatch lines, and produced one of the best Miniature longs of the time, Ch. Bijou of Mallard. Miss Fardell, using the Marlenwood and Robsvarl strain, bred four champions. Mrs. Durant, using the same breeding, bred two champions. Mrs. Stevenson of the "Amoral" Kennel and other major exhibitors bred on the same lines, but there was no particular line or inbreeding to establish a strain. In the middle '50s and early '60s, Mrs. Stevenson was very successful with eight champions carrying the "Amoral" prefix.

It was not until the early '60s that the long Miniature Dachshunds started to show a pattern which has continued today. Mrs. Hall-Fletcher's "Sagittary" Kennel seemed to have been used as a base by several present day breeders in the early days of their strains. The Sagittary Kennel was based on the importations of the Dr. Blakiston and Miss New's "Taschen" blood, including the Robsvarl and Mornyvarna lines.

Mrs. Oswell and Mrs. Fielding, in particular, made use of them. Mrs. Oswell founded the Mertynabbot line by mating a small Standard long to Mrs. Hall-Fletcher's Pluto Sagittary and bred Belita of Mertynabbot. Belita, bred to her grandson, Black Ace of Mertynabbot, produced a litter

Ch. Delphik Debbret; owner Mrs. Fielding. Photo by Diane Pearce.

of which two bitches were important: Charlotte of Mertynabbot and Byworth Carousel of Mertynabbot, sold to Mrs. King. Mrs. King mated Carousel to Marlenwood Duke Anton, a descendant of Ch. Robsvarl Red Robin, and produced Ch. Mertynabbot Byworth Comet who was bought by Mrs. Oswell. Comet, bred to his dam's sister, Charlotte of Mertynabbot, produced Ch. Mertynabbot Birthday Present. Mrs. Oswell then bought Ch. Joy of Sagittary from Mrs. Hall-Fletcher and mated her to Comet, the result being Ch. M. Little Model. This strain is now established and Comet's children and grandchildren include Ch. M. Nicola, Ch. M. Lancelot and Ch. M. Kind Sir. Lancelot is owned by Mrs. Blandford and is by Ch. Wenbarn Perigrine out of a daughter of Comet.

Mrs. Parsons, another successful breeder, came to Great Britain from India and, in the '60s, had her first success with stock going back to the Robsvarl strain. Her first champion was Minutist Storm, and one of her most beautiful dogs was Ch. Minutist Hooligan. His sire, Ch. Minutist Mikado, was also the sire of Ch. Minutist Praline and Ch. Minutist Sophistication. Her latest champion in 1971 is Ch. Minutist Eldorado.

The most successful kennel today is the Delphik Kennel of Mr. and Mrs. Fielding. Although quite successful with Miniature longs in the '50s, their real success came with the purchasing and mating of Delphik Lisba Yvonne to Reedscottage Rattan, a son of Ch. Moselle von Walder. The result was to bring the "Delphik" prefix to the forefront of the Miniature longs, for the litter contained Ch. Delphik Derry and Ch. Delphik Dhobi. Ch. Derry became the sire of eight English champions. When inbred to his daughter Della, who carried Mertynabbot blood, he produced Ch. Delphik Dekosi and Ch. Delphik Donomos, and then to another daughter, Delta, he produced Ch. Delphik Dario, Derry was also mated to a Rigalong bitch bought from Mrs. Hart—her name was Rigalong Galaxy, an offspring of Comet—producing Ch. Delphik Dodonna. Mrs. Fielding has since carried on her success by breeding in and to these lines. Most notable has been her Ch. Delphik Debbret, the result of mating Ch. Delphik Donomos to Ch. Derry's sister, Ch. Delphik Dhobi. Debbret which won thirty-five challenge certificates in twenty-two months, is the winner of the "Jackdaw" Trophy, awarded by the Dachshund Club for the top winning Dachshund of all varieties. Debbret is at present nursing a litter by their latest champion, Ch. Delphik Diplomatic, a son of Derry and Dekozi.

Derry, used by Mrs. Green to strengthen her Brigmerston Kennel, was most outstanding in siring dogs like Ch. Brigmerston Sir Francis and his son, Ch. Brigmerston Lord Charles of Primrosepatch, owned by Mrs.

Mr. Malcolm McGregor of Australia is pictured here judging the Longhaired Dachshund Club Show in the Alexandra Palace in London, July 30, 1966. The red Miniature Longhaired bitch Ch. Trumond Truella was awarded Best in Show. Breeder-owner Mr. and Mrs. F. F. Thomas. Photo by Pamela Braund.

Leonore Loeb Adler presents trophies to Miss K. Raine's Standard Wire-Haired Dachshund Imber the Baker's Man, who took reserve BIS at the Longhaired Dachshund Club Show at the Alexandra Palace, July 30, 1966. Photo by Pamela Braund.

Sedgwick, the niece of Mrs. Smith-Rewse. (Mrs. Sedgwick is carrying on the prefix.) Notable kennels breeding back to the aforementioned lines include Mrs. Fraser-Gibson's "Sunara" Kennel, Mrs. Connel's "von Holzner," Mrs. Moon's "Woodreed," Mrs. Urwin's "Urdac" and others.

WIREHAIRED MINIATURE DACHSHUNDS

The beginning of Miniature wires in England was when a few enthusiasts imported stock in the late '40s and early '50s. The "Hunterbroad" prefix of Mr. and Mrs. Maloney seems to have been based on small stock from the St. Georg and Storm Kennels, the base of Standard wire kennels prior to World War II. They imported Barro aus dem Weidmannshause and Aggi, a silver dapple wire. Mated together they produced a litter in which was Hunterbroad Graphite, who appears in practically all Miniature wire pedigrees. Barro was mated to Mrs. Besson's small Standard wire bitch, Jeda of Ballyteckel, who was line bred to Int. Ch. Wizden Sports Primavera of Seton. A daughter from this line was mated to Graphite; and a son, in turn, was mated to a bitch of Mrs. Beeson's descended from the Dunkerque wire strain on one side and from Barro on the other. This produced the first Miniature wirehaired champion, Ch. Coobeg Ballyteckel Walt Weevil, bought by Mrs. Rhodes. A bitch from this litter became the foundation bitch of Mrs. Hood-Wright's "Selwood" wire Miniatures, the most notable being Ch. Selwood Marguerite.

Rigol Kelvindeugh Painted Lady; breeder Veronica Collins; owner Anneliese Wurm. (Kennel vom Fürstenfels, Germany). Photo by Anneliese Wurm.

Meanwhile, a number of wire Miniatures evolved through the use of Standard wires and Miniature smooths, as seen in Mrs. Wakefield's first Miniature wire bitch champion, Ch. Jane of Silwood. Her sire, Liseson of Silwood, was a smooth Miniature, and Ch. Minivale Marte of Silwood was twice his granddam. Jane's dam was Selwood Paula of Dunkerque, by a smooth Miniature born of a wire Standard. In the late '50s, Group Captain and Mrs. Satchell imported Orkneyinga Jockele vom Fürstenfels, and mated him to Hunterbroad Harriet, a bitch from the Barro ex Jeda mating. A dog from this litter, Orkneyinga Oscar, was mated to a small wire Standard, Simonswood Sylphine and begot Ch. Orkneyinga Nerrina. From Harriet, mated to a grandson of the imported Aly von Sager Meer, they bred Ch. Orkneyinga Nutshell.

A successful sire in the early '60s was Ballyteckel Peter Pest, owned by Mrs. Quicke. He was from the "Huntersbroad" and "Ballyteckel" prefixes; and when bred to wire Standard lines, he produced Ch. Gisbourne Polka Dot and Ch. Gisbourne Petite Point which were both sold to Mrs. Wilson. Another daughter was Ch. Petite Poupe of Kavmar, bred and owned by Mrs. Hone; here again the dam was wire Standard bred.

Mrs. de Bernes has had much success with her "Rigol" prefix. Graphite was mated to his sister and a dog from this litter was mated to a daughter of Graphite, producing a litter in which was Redenhall Silver Wings and Redenhall Gold Braid. Redenhall Silver Wings mated to Orkneyinga/

Ch. Flaunden Wimpole Street; owner Mrs. Blandford. Photo by Diane Pearce.

Ballyteckel lines producing Rigol Phantom Philip, a silver dapple wire who sired Ch. Rigol Phantom Phoebe, and also the first dapple wire Miniature champion, Kelvindeugh Lauder Likely, owned by Mrs. Collins. Mrs. de Bernes is now residing in France.

Squadron Leader and Mrs. Whitehouse were very successful with Redenhall Gold Braid. They mated him to Paulette of Silwood, which they had bought from Mrs. Wakefield, and bred three champions—Ch. Gold Bracken of Granta, Ch. Teak of Granta and Ch. Gold Ilex of Granta. On the untimely death of Mrs. Whitehouse, the kennel was taken over by Mrs. Blandford of the "Flaunden" prefix. She had bred several champions from this line, notable Ch. Flauden the Whitehouse and her latest, Ch. Flaunden Wimpole Street.

Mrs. Howard had some excellent results by mating the Huntersbroad, through Redenhall Gauntlet, into her own wire Standards, producing Ch. O'Kay of Seale and Ch. Omah of Seale. Mrs. Willoughby has managed to keep this line through Witch of Seale, producing Ch. Witch Doctor of Seale. Mrs. Spong had success by mating Orkneyinga Nereid, a sister of Ch. Orkneyinga Nutshell, to the wire Miniature, Merryweather Moustachio. A son of this litter, Ch. Peredur Pimento, was inbred back to his dam and the result was Ch. Peredur Sinful Skinful. Pimento was the sire of three champions, but the real influence was through the sister of Pimento. Ch.

Wee Taffy of Paxford, bought by Miss Gray and mated to Ch. Redenhall Yewberry.

Yewberry was bred by Mr. Colbourne and was descended from Walt Weevil on his dam's side and on his sire's side was a grandson of the smooth Miniature, Ch. Flaunden Senator. Yewberry was also the sire of Mrs. Green's Ch. Daxene Black Unity; afterwards both Yewberry and Unity were bought by Mrs. Lawley. The mating of Yewberry to Wee Taffy resulted in an outstanding sire, Ch. Bryn of Paxford, who won the Miniature Dachshund Club's Trophy for the best stud dog in all coats for the years 1969 and 1970. Mr. Smith bought a bitch by Pimento and took her to Yewberry, producing Ch. Silvae the Mouse, bought by Mrs. Grosvenor Workman. Ch. Bryn of Paxford was also the sire of Mrs. Grosvenor Workman's latest Ch. Silvae Enormouse, Miss Harriman's Ch. Vienda Live Wire and Miss Raphael's Ch. Andyc Topper and Ch. Andyc Tansy, with more young stock winning in the showring today.

GENERAL INFORMATION ON ALL VARIETIES

It is possible at this moment for a Dachshund to be registered at the English Kennel Club by the breed which its coat and size resembles, but this is subject to review in 1976. This means it is possible to mate a Miniature long to a Standard wire and to register the result as a Miniature smooth without any query being made by the English Kennel Club. To become a champion, it is necessary to win three challenge certificates under three different judges. The challenge certificate is won by the best dog and the best bitch; although puppies can win challenge certificates, it is now necessary to win at least one when over twelve months old. In Miniature wires, when challenge certificates were first allocated to the breed, the weight was twelve pounds. The weight is now reduced to eleven pounds to coincide with the Miniature smooths and Miniature longs. Until three years ago, the judging points included the words "The ideal weight is from 7–9 lbs." but these words have been deleted. At a recent meeting of the Miniature Dachshund Club, it was decided that, in view of the alteration of the weight in the U.S.A. from nine pounds to ten pounds, the special classes which had always been included at their shows for under nine pounds only now have classes for under ten pounds. In 1967 a Dachshund Council was formed comprising all the English and Scottish Dachshund Clubs; this council is referred to when a kennel club nominates judges and expresses an opinion as to the nominated judges' ability to judge all varieties of Dachshund. The Council issues its Judging List to all Dachshund and general championship shows. This is not the Kennel Club official list, but should be used as a guide by the show committees. The Council is the medium through which any Dachshund club can have interclub matters discussed and sent to the Kennel Club for consideration.

A GLIMPSE AT AUSTRALIAN DACHSHUNDS

Some time ago, Mr. C. A. Binney, secretary of the Kennel Club in London, Great Britain, wrote in private correspondence that the standard for the six varieties of Dachshunds recognized by the Kennel Club is also valid in Australia.

Though we have no "official" Australian Report, we do have some photos of longhaired Standard Dachshunds, sent to me by Mr. and Mrs. Harry Jay of Black Rock, Victoria. Mrs. Jay wrote that the Australian Dachshunds are descendants of English stock, and, therefore, resemble that type. *L.L.A.*

Longlo Black Godiva is mother to Harca Purzel. Their owner is Mrs. Cassia Jay of Victoria. Photo by Harry Jay.

"Purzel" grew sad and lonely after her mother "Blackie" died, so a new three-month-old puppy, Hoylace Biddy, was given to her as a companion. Owner Mrs. Cassia Jay. Photo by Harry Jay.

REMARKS
ON CANADIAN DACHSHUNDS

By Sarah Diamond

(Director of the Canadian Kennel Club; Chairman of the Judge's Committee; Chairman of the Registration Committee.)

In Canada there are six breeds of Dachshunds—three coats in Standard Dachshunds, and three coats in Miniature Dachshunds (not over nine pounds). Of these six, each breed has its own championship points; yet while it seldom happens, all six breeds are eligible to compete in the Group at championship shows.

Coats and sizes may not be interbred. Any Miniature weighed at a championship show and found to be over nine pounds is excused from competition.

All dogs are registered through the Registration Division of the Canadian Kennel Club, which is governed by the Live Stock Pedigree Act, and any breeder who falsifies a pedigree, alters a registration certificate, sells an unidentified animal as Pure-bred, or sells without supplying registration papers, is liable to a fine of $50.00 to $500.00, or to be imprisoned for a term not exceeding two months.

All Pure-bred dogs must be either tattooed or nose printed by the breeder, with most breeders choosing tattooing, as this method allows for instant identification. An allotment of letters is supplied to the breeder by the Registration Division of the Canadian Kennel Club, and these letters are used on all dogs bred by the breeder. He or she also adds a number for each dog, followed by another specified letter to indicate the year of birth. Tattooing can be done on the ear, flank or lips. The ear is usually chosen for most breeds, but those with standing or cropped ears are tattooed on the flank.

Those who wish to nose print, a method usually used for adult dogs, obtain nose print forms from the Canadian Kennel Club; two of these forms with legible prints are required with each application for registration.

All Canadian breeders are required to keep records of their breeding program which can be examined at any time.

An American exhibitor wishing to show a Miniature Dachshund at a Canadian show, may request the show superintendent to officially weigh the dog and record the weight on an official Canadian Kennel Club form. The

Audrey McNaughton's rendition of retired Ch. Di-Mar's Wee Gemini, top winning smooth Miniature Dachshund in 1967 and 1968. Owner Sarah Diamond of Canada.

Mrs. Sarah Diamond of Quebec, Canada, with three of her Miniature Dachshunds. From left to right: Ch. Di-Mar's Wee Gemini, his daughter, Ch. Di-Mar's Wee Shouma, and Ch. Di-Mar's Wee Tornado. Photo by Irving Diamond.

Miniature Dachshund must be over one year of age and not over nine pounds.

To register a dog born in a foreign country, this "recent" certificate of weighing must be sent with application form and nose prints, to the Registration Division of the Canadian Kennel Club, 2, Eva Road, Etobicoke, Ontario.

No dog will be confirmed as a Canadian Champion until registered in our records.

Canadian Ch. Wilheen's Lady Marion M.W., 4th in Group under Judge Irving Diamond, bred by Dr. and Mrs. Wm. C. Adams of California and co-owned by the breeders and Mrs. Joyce Alden of Ontario, Canada. Handler Andre Jeannette. Photo by Wainwright.

Canadian Ch. Lenair's Longjohn, Canada's Top Dachshund All Coats for 1969, was judged under Maxwell Riddle and co-owned by Mr. and Mrs. O. R. Langford of Ontario, Canada. Handler Mrs. Helen Langford. Dog was "Best Canadian Bred in Show." Photo by Ed. Beaulieu.

Five Generations of Miniature Smooth Champions. Owner Mrs. Sarah Diamond. Ch. Magic Gift of Seale (Eng. Import), mother; Ch. Di-Mar's Black Satin, daughter; Ch. Di-Mar's Frolic, granddaughter; Ch. Di-Mar's Frolicsome, great-granddaughter; Ch. Di-Mar's Wee Nosegay, great-great-granddaughter. Photo by A. Crombie McNeill.

HISTORY OF THE DACHSHUND CLUB
OF AMERICA
Compiled by John Hutchinson Cook
(Judge of many different breeds; former President of D.C.A.; currently director of D.C.A.)

The first eleven Dachshunds were registered between 1879 and 1885. The Dachshund Club of America was recognized as a member club by the American Kennel Club in 1895. The first president of the DCA was Mr. Harry Peters (Sr.). The club was incorporated in New York State in 1932. The Breed Standard (present) was adopted by the DCA and approved by the AKC in 1935.

The first big independent Specialty Show was held 1934 in New York; Mrs. Tainter judged an entry of 204. Between 1936–41 specialties were held at the Morris & Essex Shows. There were big entries under German judges: Mr. Marquard judged an entry of 276; Mr. Ströh judged an entry of 311. The 50th Anniversary Specialty Show was held in New York, and Mr. Horswell judged an entry of 284. In 1960, the DCA membership voted to alternate locations of the independent Specialty Shows yearly between

Ch. Lynsulee's Luckibelle is the dam of nine champions. Here she is judged by John Hutchinson Cook and handled by owner Philip S. Bishop of Ohio. Photo by Ludwig.

64

metropolitan New York City and the West: Chicago, Ill., 1961; New York, N.Y., 1962; Del Monte, Calif., 1963; New York, N.Y., 1964; etc. The high point was reached in 1963 with an entry of 314, judged by Mrs. Van Court and myself. Entries at specialties have thus risen from 57 in 1931 to 246 in 1964.

The earliest independent Regional Specialty Show was organized in California. Others, which followed were: Heart of America (St. Louis), Pennsylvania, Midwest (Detroit), Central States (Chicago)—now inactive, and others. Currently they number approximately 45, a few are inactive, but new ones are added every year. In 1963 about 38 Regional Specialty Shows were held.

Individual Dachshund registrations by the American Kennel Club have continued to rise:

1930—166 were registered—27th place of all breeds of dogs
1938—3,213 were registered—7th place of all breeds of dogs
1946—6,598 were registered—6th place of all breeds of dogs
1955—26,026 were registered—5th place of all breeds of dogs
1964—48,569 were registered—4th place of all breeds of dogs
1970—61,042 were registered—third place in all breeds of dogs.

The number of Dachshunds registered by A.K.C. increased considerably since 1964, as listed above. And at the same time Dachshund popularity moved up to third place out of 116 A.K.C. registered breeds listed for 1970.

In 1970 the Dachshund Club of America's 75th Anniversary Specialty Show was held in New York. The judges were Mr. and Mrs. Fred Heying of California. Rose Heying judged 149 Smooth Dachshunds and the Inter-Variety Competition at the end of the regular single coat competitions. Fred Heying judged 61 Wirehaired and 113 Longhaired Dachshunds. Including 18 Dachshunds listed for the "Parade of Veterans" and 4 for "Exhibition only" there was a total of 345 Dachshunds entered.

Early in 1971 the Board of Directors of the American Kennel Club approved a revision of the Dachshund Standard of Perfection. The D.C.A. membership had approved the revisions in a mail vote taken in the fall of 1969. The two major changes were regarding (1) dew claws, which may be removed; and (2) Miniature Dachshunds, concerning their maximum weight in the show ring. "They have not been given separate classification, but are a division of the Open Class for 'under 10 pounds, and 12 months old or over.' "

It is notable, also, that the language has been radically changed: no longer is the passage on Miniature Dachshunds a translation of the German standard with its chest measurements. The text is now short, precise, and to the point.

Chapter II
Breed Characteristics

Anyone who has followed the history of the Dachshund carefully will have noticed that the concept of the breed is not a primitive or natural development, but rather an artificial and a willful one. The *Tachskriecher* (the little badger dog) varied considerably in structure over the course of several centuries before reaching the modern Dachshund type. Sometimes it was reminiscent of a Spaniel type dog; sometimes it was similar to the later Pinscher or Terrier types. At other times it resembled variously small *Tieflaufhunden* ("low-legged dogs") and *Niederbracken* ("low-bracken," several types of low proto-Dachshunds). Then again it favored the slight and low *Leithunden* ("guide dogs") and especially the small *Gebirgsschweisshunden* ("mountain bloodhounds").

But always—and this alone was and is the essence of the breed, and it

Ch. Jo-Del's Nicholas and the sponsors of his triumphs, Dr. Betty-Jo Koss (who is being nuzzled) and Dolores J. Farley (who conducts him in his superb ring appearances). "Jo-Del" was retired after winning his 25th BIS at the age of six years and six months. He is owned jointly by Dr. Koss and Miss Farley, both of Indiana. Photo by Ritter.

must remain so—they were small dogs with pronounced aggressiveness in the presence of game. Everything else, namely what we understand as the features of the "Breed Standard" was and is, more or less, changeable and dependent upon human whims; for the essential purpose of the breed these features are mostly immaterial, even at times deleterious.

They concern secondary values only, which are raised to be breed characteristics whenever a large group of people, usually directed by a few "leaders," so pleases. But they do not mean anything with respect to the original essence of the "breed." Herein lies the source of the more or less important faults, which we call the trends of the fashion in the breed. As Jungklaus, M.D., PH.D., an ornithologist and hunting dog specialist, so strikingly stated: the origin of these faults lies in establishing canonically a momentary condition, without regard to its source, i.e., its initial state; ignorant people then may get the impression that the "official standard" includes points—even though these are actually new—belonging to the intrinsic and original, and, at the same time, unchangeable essence of the breed. Next, it poses the question, how much does the standard really reflect the actual facts, or does it simply represent the opinion of a few or of many breeders.

Let us discuss first what is meant by an accepted trend in fashion. It is in no way wholly dependent upon its usefulness to the breed, even though it often gives this appearance. In Dachshunds, to give an example, the shape of the ear has no practical importance; indeed, its modern length has more disadvantages in fights with game than advantages; there cannot be any dispute on this account. A gentleman once tried to explain that the "deeper meaning" of the exaggerated long and broad ears was a protection of the carotid artery from predatory game. Yet the "unprotected" carotid of a Fox Terrier or a fox has never been reported as particularly prone to injury. Such a possibility in fact for anatomical reasons, would be almost impossible.

In earlier centuries Dachshunds had straight legs. Then appeared the "typical digging legs" with which it was more difficult for Dachshunds to dig than it was before. For a long time, one almost saw only Dachshunds with definitely turned out front feet. Here and there this trend was opposed repeatedly in breed publications—and rightfully so. The fashionable crooked Dachshund legs of that time became gradually old-fashioned. And in 1920 Pohlmey stated: "In Berlin they don't want any more crooked legs now!" Earlier, in 1912, Löns wrote: "The accepted standard asserts that the Dachshund is an earthdog; and the stretched-out, long-legged build of the Dachshund is the best and most suitable body for work under the earth. This view, though, has been refuted long ago by the fact that higher legs and a shorter body afford the dog a much greater agility and strength also below the earth; as is seen in the fox who is long-legged (as well as in Fox Terriers who are excellent crawlers)."

"Therefore the 'Dachshund shape' is not in the least favorable for work inside the den; it is also not the origin of its peculiar build. Would the performance inside the den have been made the basis of the breed, then the Dachshund body would soon disappear."

The breeding of domestic animals which are not exclusively raised for a utilitarian purpose falls under the dangerous influence of fashion, which itself succumbs easily to whims and notions. Fickle ideals of beauty and the mood of individual influential personalities then dictate only too readily

Ch. Lynsulee's Buckeye Bird shown here by owner-handler Philip S. Bishop of Ohio under judge Dr. Lyman Fisher. Photo by Norton of Kent.

"the" breed characteristics. Breed characteristics, to repeat once more, are not given in an absolute sense; they are not things in themselves. But instead, they are something subjectively human, something flexible. It may be that to some these clarifications seem too "philosophical." Yet they are absolutely necessary as a guide through this maze, especially for the thoughtful practitioner.

There is still another preliminary point that seems important to discuss.

Whoever wants to devote himself to breeding any dog breed must absolutely understand that while man may love a breed, nature at the same time appears to hate it. If the breeder does not select again and again, the type is lost through the forces of nature. If all puppies of every litter would be used again for breeding without selection, then it would become apparent that in a great number of offspring the fine points of the breed would soon be lost—even if they had been purebred for decades before. The reason for this happening lies in the fact that the breeds we raise are not natural breeds. All artificial breeds have the tendency to revert to the original type or types of the canines. This in itself explains why a breeder has to expect deviations from a fine point of the breed, even with the best of purebred strains. Furthermore, it is true that, without exception, each breed carries, more or less, blood of other breeds. These bloodlines breaking through become noticeable, again and again, in the outward appearance. It might have been that these different bloodlines were introduced by chance or on purpose, consciously or without knowledge. And it is especially our Dachshund who carries a good bit of alien blood. This statement is surely not meant as a reproach, for these infusions have often brought him numerous advantages. For the wirehaired Dachshund we have to thank, to a great extent, the influx of German wirehaired Pinscher blood and the bloodlines of English

Ch. Westphal's Wandering Wind here winning Hound Group 1, under judge Mrs. Robert Tongren. Co-owners Mrs. Richard Lang and Mrs. Dorothy S. Pickett of Connecticut, who is the handler. Photo by Evelyn M. Shafer.

wirehaired terriers, Scottish, Skye, and especially the Dandie Dinmont. As such, the wirehaired variety is one of the keenest and best of the Dachshunds. Often the overbred smooth Dachshund turned out to be too thinly coated, afraid of water, and sickly. Undoubtedly, by the introduction of new blood, they received an additional measure of alertness, intelligence, ability to work in any weather, and enjoyment of water-work. In earlier decades Black-and-Tan (Manchester) Terrier blood was occasionally introduced to achieve a more distinctive marking, a more graceful tail, and a more alert disposition. Besides, Dachshund blood was frequently supplemented by that of Wachtelhunds and Spaniels, an infusion which, to a larger extent, led to the modern reëstablishment of the longhaired Dachshund variety.

Here and there in the mountains, Dachsbracken blood was used to produce a more robust type. It was especially after the 1848 Revolution that "Bloodhound" (see earlier discussion of "Bloodhounds" in Chapter One) lines were mixed with Dachshund blood, frequently on purpose, and

Ch. Nixon's Penthouse Spreena; judge William S. Houpt. Owner-handler Howard Atlee of New York. Photo by Evelyn M. Shafer.

Ch. Benmarden's Anna Mae W.; judge Dr. Lyman R. Fisher. Owner
Evelyn E. Wray; handler Woody Pflueger. Photo by Earl Graham.

occasionally unintentionally. Particularly in the Harz, but also in other
mountain ranges, the forestry rangers kept practically only Dachshunds
and Bloodhounds. In this way it was not at all rare that unintentional cross-
breeding occurred between these two breeds, which were so closely related
in blood, color, type, and hunting ability (dependability on the trail, as well
as keenness). These crosses concerned the red-coated type of both breeds,
although black-and-tan Bloodhounds occurred also. Occasionally there were
both dappled Dachshunds and Bloodhounds, but the red color of both
breeds predominated in the mountain regions. With full justification we
speak, even today, of the Dachshund, the red in particular, as the little
Bloodhound. In fact, that is just the capacity in which they are used in those
parts of the mountains where the large Bloodhounds are no longer kept
because of lack of work and food. Years ago in the Harz and in the Eichsfelde
it was not rare to see Dachshunds who undoubtedly carried Bloodhound
lines, as certainly nobody denied. On the contrary, people were rather

71

proud of this fact, because Dachshunds with Bloodhound blood were supposed to have special advantages and were paid well. Dark masks on red Dachshunds were well liked and valued; they looked rather good, too. The ancestors of the superb red Dachshund strain bred by the von Daackes were said to have had quite a few drops of Bloodhound blood.

There are no other hunting dog breeds to which Dachshunds are more closely related than to the Bloodhounds. This is true for all main points of conformation—the comparative length and low build; shape of head, tail, and bone structure—and character traits such as keenness and dependability on the trail. It would be no great trick to breed a Dachshund type out of some of the Bloodhound lines, especially since many lines carried some Dachshund blood ever since the 1850's. One of the best connoisseurs of the Dachshund and the light Mountain Bloodhound, Chief Forestry Administrator Volkmar, of Pfünz (Bavaria), stated: "Mountain people were never exacting: Dachshund, Bloodhound, Niederlaufhund, etc., they mixed the blood frequently, and just took things in their stride."

A beginner in the Dachshund breed must consider this fact, so that he knows the causes of the variability within the breed, which can explain aberrant puppies which do occur from time to time. Connected therewith also

Ch. Debbie V. Wanderlust (top winning Wire Bitch in 1965); judge Charles Kellog. Owner Mrs. Lois de W. Shabatura of Minnesota; handler Eugene H. Shabatura. Photo by Jean A. Whitesell.

Ch. Desert Herman the Great VII; judge Dr. Frank R. Booth. Owner Jane K. Wolfinger of Nevada, handler Garland A. Baker. Photo by Morry Twomey.

are seemingly unexplainable throwbacks, which at times created some justified sensation. So it was with the magnificent longhaired Dachshund "Schlupp-Saarau," with his excellent coat, color, and build. He repeatedly received the highest prizes for the best Dachshund of all classes at all the biggest exhibitions. For quite a while he dominated the entire longhaired variety. He possessed an excellent and far-reaching pedigree of the best red Dachshunds—but all his ancestors, as far as it was known, were pure smooths. He also had a longhaired brother, "Lump-Saarau." Repeated good longhaired "chance products" also came from the "Hundesports Waldmann" line, without anybody ever knowing where the longhaired blood came from. "Waldmann v. Thal" and "Waldine du Nord" frequently had longhaired offspring. Some point to "Flott-Sonnenberg" for this blood. A breeder always has to be prepared for such reverses due to some unknown bloodlines far back in the pedigree, despite all the best "pure" breeding. Different coat varieties, body shapes, and long forgotten colors, as white paws, half-white legs, white blaze on the forehead, and white spots on the chest and throat, like one sometimes finds on Dachsbracken, are liable to appear. One would see them much more frequently, if the breeder would not quickly and quietly, in false shame, kill these dogs. Nothing, however, would be more interesting genetically than to raise these "chance products" and then to mate them with related dogs. In this way one could study the essence of the breed and its origin (or better, its origins). One would surely achieve the most remarkable results by the fourth or fifth generation.

Ch. Penthouse Salome. Judge William Hackett. Owner Howard Atlee of New York. Handler Robert Fowler. Photo by William P. Gilbert.

Ch. Holow's Christopher L. Judge Robert Waters. Owner Wilfred E. Boyer of Maryland. Handler Bobby Barlow. Photo by Morry Twomey.

Ch. Von Relgib's Red Witch. Judge Louie Grugette. Co-owners Herbert and Elaine Holtzman of California. Handler Woody Dorward. Photo by Ludwig.

Tanga-Ta Rebel Yell. Judge John Hutchinson Cook. Co-owners James and Irene Swyler of Virginia. Handler Irene Swyler. Photo by Ritter.

These general observations were necessary here to prepare the beginner as much as possible, in order for him to engage in the study of the breed characteristics without prejudice.

We have seen that breed concepts have changed much over the passing of the years. We have seen that the concept of the breed is an artificial one, created by man's whim. We have seen that breed characteristics are much more dependent upon fashion and the opinion of some prominent dog breeders than usefulness or physiological necessity.

The practical and independent person has to accept these facts from the start, even though he has misgivings about some of the "breed characteristics."

It is frequently not the breed characteristics themselves which are rightfully criticized, but their definition and exaggerated interpretation! For instance, when the standard mentions that Dachshunds should be long and low, it by no means refers to dogs with *exaggerated* length and lowness.

In other words, the importance assigned to different aspects of the standard differs. This fact explains why even highly regarded stock will be

Ch. Lynsulee's Randy; judge Larry Krebs. Owner-handler Philip Bishop of Ohio. Photo by Norton of Kent.

Ch. Scarlet Cedar's Licorice; judge Maurice L. Baker. Co-owners Chester and Dore Leiser of Colorado; handler Dorothy McNulty. Photo by Morry Twomey.

rated differently by various judges. The hunter will judge the dog's appearance from a more practical point of view. The show judge (with respect to the fancy) will be more inclined toward an exaggerated interpretation, which in the extreme may result in a caricature of the original. However, these are human foibles which probably will never disappear completely.

Löns expressed this sentiment in pamphlet No. 26, *Deutsche Gesellschaft für Züchtungskunde* ("German Association for the Science of Breeding"): "The unspoiled Dachshund fancier looks in his darling for a small, highly elegant, mischievous and really beautiful Dachshund; he does not want to show a caricature, who was bred for a few single exaggerated points which are valued above all else. Even the most obdurate breeder, indeed, holds this ideal close to his heart. Such feelings come to light whenever a really symmetrically built, beautiful Dachshund appears, who is also good in the desirable main characteristics without any exaggerations."

These facts cannot be stressed strongly enough in the interest of the future of the Dachshund breed.

Some breeders, judges, and "experts" apply a similar measure for evaluation of the Dachshund, and for the dog in general, as they do, justifiably, for the horse. The horse is bred for speed, especially on open, flat ground, or for packing or pulling a load. Therefore it needs a firm, strongly-built, and heavy-boned structure. In many ways the dog's duties are exactly the opposite. He must be agile and flexible, his ligaments stretchable and pliable like those of his ancestors. Only in this manner can the dog adapt as the wolf adapts to his environment, as when he has to squeeze through thickets and clefts in rocks or to overcome quickly and safely the hazards of steep mountainsides, such as falling or rolling rocks. The stiff, tightly muscled, and heavy-boned horse is never capable of performing such feats. Nor can it crawl or creep like the agile dog, whose muscles, tendons, ligaments, and joints are not slack but elastic and yielding, or should be so. A healthy sprightly horse always stands taut, and always posed. Even the best dog, however, can look from one moment to another "advantageous" or "disadvantageous." Observing him sufficiently long at rest, one can catch him momentarily in all sorts of "faulty" poses, with faults which, in reality, he does not have. Such is seldom the case with stiff dogs, which are built like horses.

Let us turn now to a consideration of the specific breed characteristics:

I.—GENERAL FEATURES*

General Appearance—*Low to ground, short-legged, long-bodied, but with compact figure and robust muscular development; with bold and confident carriage of the head and intelligent facial expression.*

In spite of his shortness of leg, in comparison with his length of trunk, he should appear neither crippled, awkward, cramped in his capacity for movement nor slim and weasel-like.

The Dachshund's appearance must show at first glance that he is made for his work, below and above the earth: he must be small enough to work nimbly in a tight den and agile enough to search with perseverance in difficult territory and keep to the blood-trail. In comparison with other breeds, the Dachshund looks stretched-out and short-legged. Though both of these characteristics are not necessary for work below the earth, as can be seen in the fox and Fox Terrier, as long as these features do not exceed

---

* In the section on breed characteristics, paragraphs in italics are reprinted by courtesy of the Dachshund Club of America, from the "Official Breed Standard for Dachshunds," as adopted by the Dachshund Club of America and approved by the Board of Directors of the American Kennel Club. February, 1971

moderate limits, they are no hindrance; instead, they add to the characteristic appearance of the Dachshund. They are also useful for deliberate, unrelenting pursuit and low search work. However, a lack of proportion between the limbs and the long body should by all means be avoided. The Dachshund ideal should give the impression of a small, refined, proportioned build, free from any caricature.

The male should have a more robust build, a more massive head, a more compact appearance than the bitch, who should have a slighter head, a more slender appearance, and be more supple in essence.

The stature should be long and vigorous, never plump and clumsy, nor weasel-like and weak; the deportment should be sprightly and challenging, with a keen and intelligent expression.

Different types of dogs for work in dens.

Qualities—*He should be clever, lively and courageous to the point of rashness, persevering in his work both above and below ground; with all the senses well developed. His build and disposition qualify him especially for hunting game below ground.*

Added to this, his hunting spirit, good nose, loud tongue, and small size, render him especially suited for beating the bush.

His figure and fine nose give him an especial advantage over most other breeds of sporting dogs for trailing.

The Dachshund should be fiery, persevering, and dashing, droll in play, and untiring. By nature he is mostly headstrong and moody, with tender care he responds by being faithful and attached, obedient and trainable. In any case the Dachshund is in essence one of the most peculiar dogs, almost like a cross between friendliness and rudeness, high spirit and weariness, thirst for activity and laziness, equanimity and sensitivity, diminutiveness and megalomania. These paradoxes can be explained because this dog was coddled and spoiled and yet had to perform the most independent and most difficult tasks below the earth. All his senses are well developed, especially his sense of smell. According to these characteristics, the Dachshund should not only be typical, but, above all, he should be purposeful; he should be agile, dry, tenacious, and enduring in his build, and therefore never too low, dragging to the ground, too lank or too plump, neither weasel-like nor turtle-like, instead he should "stand firmly on the ground."

Skeleton—The bones should not be distended, spongy, or, even perhaps, rickety, but should be strong, of a hard, dense consistency. Quality breeding produces firmer structure and refinement of exterior lines. Overbreeding, however, leads to loosening up of body tissues, to swelling and sponginess. (Compare the domestic duck with the wild duck, the domestic pig with the wild boar.) In judging the Dachshund skeleton, one should especially be sure that the spine in the lumbar region is not noticeably curved inward or depressed, as otherwise a sagging back or, even worse, a sway-back results, which is equally as ugly as it is an impediment. The absolutely straight back, or "cow back," is also anatomically incorrect and disadvantageous. On photos, however, it is often only the result of retouching by unversed artists. The upper extensions of the vertebrae (spinous process) must be sufficiently long to permit ample room for attachment of the musculature. Equally so, the shoulder blade should be big and broad to offer sufficient surface for attachment of powerful muscles. Similar considerations hold true for the pelvic bones; the bones of the extremities; and especially the jaw bones, where the musculature must be well developed, for the dog must not only use these bones to grasp game but also to hold them long enough. The ribs should form a sufficiently large chest, which along its lower line (thorax) presents an even oval outline. This line, therefore, must not have a sharp break (discontinuous chest line) or an angular continuity, otherwise the thorax might impede mobility in tight tunnels.

Conformation of Body—Head: *Viewed from above or from the side, it should taper uniformly to the tip of the nose, and should be clean cut.*

The skull is only slightly arched and should slope gradually without stop (the less stop, the more typical) into the finely-formed slightly-arched muzzle (ram's nose). The bridge bones over the eyes should be strongly prominent.

The nasal cartilage and tip of the nose are long and narrow, lips tightly stretched, well covering the lower jaw, but neither deep nor pointed, corner of the mouth not very marked. Nostrils well opened.

Jaws opening wide and hinged well back of the eyes, with strongly developed bones and teeth.

Head: clear-cut. Lips should be tightly drawn so as not to offer any surface area for assault. Corners of the mouth slightly marked. Form of head long, conical in shape and finely cut. Upper skull not too broad, but neither too narrow. The muzzle, the jaws, should not be too narrow and too fine or Greyhound-like, but neither should they be too short and too blunt

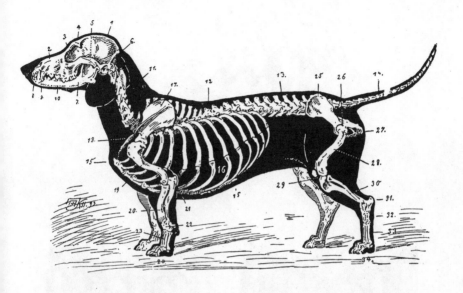

The skeleton of the Dachshund. 1. Occiput; 2. Muzzle; 3. Eye socket; 4. Forehead; 5. Upper jawbone; 6. Base of skull; 7. Lower jaw; 8. Incisors (scissors bite); 9. Canine teeth; 10. Molars; 11. Cervical vertebrae (seven); 12. Thoracic vertebrae(thirteen); 13. Lumbar vertebrae (seven); 14. Caudal vertebrae; 15. Breast bone; 16. Thorax (nine fixed and 4 floating ribs); 17. Shoulder blade; 18. Shoulder; 19. Upper arm; 20. Forearm; 21. Elbow; 22. Wrist; 23. Pastern; 24. Front paw with five toes; 25. Pelvis; 26. Pelvic joint; 27. Sacro-iliac; 28. Thigh; 29. Knee, or stifle; 30. Shin; 31. Hock joint; 32. Tarsus; 33. Metatarsus; 34. Hind paw with four toes.

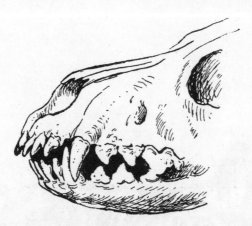

Scissors bite.

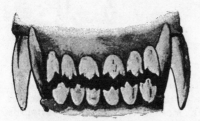

¾ to 1 ½ year old
(jagged edged incisors).

1 ½ to 2 ½ years old.

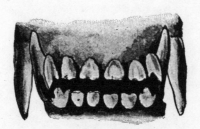

2 ½ to 3 ½ years old.

or Bloodhound-like. While a long muzzle can encompass a greater part of the adversary, by the laws of leverage it cannot grip as firmly as a shorter one. The jaws should spread wide, extending behind the eyes.

TEETH: *Powerful canine teeth should fit closely together, and the outer side of the lower incisors should tightly touch the inner side of the upper. (Scissors bite.)*

The teeth should be well developed. The strong canines must interlock perfectly. The inside of the upper incisors touches the front of the lower incisors. The pincer bite, where the upper and lower incisors meet directly, is somewhat rare and anatomically not correct. With older dogs it can be the result of worn out incisors which give the false impression of a pincer bite.

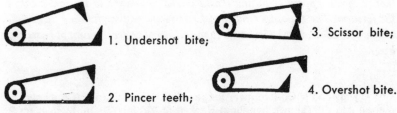

1. Undershot bite;   3. Scissor bite;

2. Pincer teeth;   4. Overshot bite.

Diagram of bite.

When, with the muzzle closed, the upper and lower incisors lie so much apart that the upper protrude from $\frac{1}{8}$ inch to $\frac{3}{8}$ inch or more, a condition called overshot bite exists. In Dachshunds this is a frequent serious fault. On the other hand, if the lower incisors protrude, then the condition is known as undershot bite. In Dachshunds this is a rarity.

EYES: *Medium size, oval, situated at the sides, with a clear, energetic though pleasant expression, not piercing. Color lustrous dark reddish-brown to brownish-black for all coats and colors.*

Wall eyes in the case of dapple dogs are not a very bad fault, but are also not desirable.

EARS: *Should be set near the top of the head, and not too far forward, long but not too long, beautifully rounded, not narrow, pointed, or folded. Their carriage should be animated, and the forward edge should just touch the cheek.*

The ears are very flexible, and when the dog's attention is aroused the cartilage at the base of the ear is moved forward and upward. Ears that are too short do not look pretty. If they are too long and broad, they offer too big a surface for assault by game, the so-called "fox-food." Medium large, sufficiently high ears, set back far enough, are least in danger. The distance between the eye and the onset of the ear should be longer than in other breeds; this feature gives the head of the Dachshund its characteristic look and protects the ears better from the bites of enemies.

NECK: *Fairly long, muscular, clean-cut, not showing any dewlap on the* throat, *slightly arched in the nape, extending in a graceful line into the shoulders, carried proudly but not stiffly.*

The neck must be sufficiently free and long so that the dog, at any gait, can sniff comfortably along the ground. This point is often neglected by dog breeders and judges because a beautiful and sufficiently long neck, held high, will make the entire dog appear higher.

Trunk—*The whole trunk should in general be long and fully muscled. The back, with sloping shoulders and short rigid pelvis, should lie in the straightest possible line between the withers and the very slightly arched loins, these latter being short, rigid and broad.*

(*a*) Chest: *The breast bone should be strong, and so prominent in front that on either side a depression (dimple) appears. When viewed from the front, the thorax should appear oval, and should extend downward to the mid-point of the forearm. The enclosing structure of ribs should appear full and oval, full-volumed, so as to allow by its ample capacity, complete development of heart and lungs.*

Ch. Wyndwood's Christopher; judge Alice Marie Cornet. Co-owned by Marian and Bill (shown handling) Hackett of Virginia. Photo by William P. Gilbert.

Ch. Doxie Belle's Penelope; judge Mrs. Ralph Levering. Owner-handler
Garland V. Bell of Virginia. Photo by Evelyn M. Shafer.

Well ribbed up, and gradually merging into the line of the abdomen.

*If the length is correct, and also the anatomy of the shoulder and upper arm,
the front leg when viewed in profile should cover the lowest point of the breast
line.*

(*b*) ABDOMEN: *Slightly drawn up.*

Many faults in Dachshunds appear in the back. It should be hard-
muscled and taut. One talks of a roach, or carp, back when the back is
curved up, and a sunken, or sway, back when it is bent in. The absolutely
straight back is, at times, a stage before the sunken back; the dog is easily
fatigued because its back lacks resiliency, and frequently the withers are not
high enough. This condition is mostly the result of the spinous processes of
the first seven vertebrae not being long enough. The beautiful, faintly
curved, taut back is the best expression of the powerful back musculature.
It serves for the transmission of movement from the hindleg to the front
leg, and therefore is of the greatest importance in the forward motion of
dogs. The Dachshund's back should be a good medium length to suit his
work below and above the ground. A back which is too short is not flexible
enough for bends in subterranean dens; a back which is too long is not as
well supported by the legs, and therefore the dog tires more easily, as one

could generally observe in old-type hunting dogs with long backs. The back can be divided into two principal parts, (1) the thorax and (2) the kidney section, including the croup. The thorax should be long in order to afford enough room for the lungs, especially since it cannot be too deep and arched; it would otherwise represent a hindrance in many dens. In comparison, the kidney section must be short, hard, and solidly muscled. Length would only be gained at the expense of the strength of the back. A certain length of thorax is more valuable than a great depth because of the little known fact that, at least in the male, breathing is of the so-called diaphragm type. In this the lungs are extended more in length, thereby pushing the intestines together to make room for the expanding lungs. In the pregnant bitch the "chest" type of breathing is more frequent than "diaphragm" breathing.

Tail—*Set in continuation of the spine and extending without very pronounced curvature, and should not be carried too gaily.*

Medium high and sturdily set in, the tail should then proceed straight and smoothly, short and Pointer-like. A short, straight, and steely tail contributes greatly to the noble general appearance of the Dachshund. Even in emotional moments it should not be carried too high. It should be well covered, but not with too coarse hair. In any case it is better to have a tail covered with coarse hair, a little longer on the underside, than to have too fine a growth of hair on a thin and what is usually a ratlike tail.

Front—*To endure the arduous exertion underground, the front must be correspondingly muscular, compact, deep, long and broad. Forequarters in detail:*

(a) SHOULDER BLADES: *Long, broad, obliquely and firmly placed upon the fully-developed thorax, furnished with hard and plastic muscles.*

(b) UPPER ARM: *Of the same length as the shoulder blade, and at right angles to the latter, strong of bone and hard of muscle, lying close to the ribs, capable of free movement.*

(c) FOREARM: *This is short in comparison to other breeds, slightly turned inwards; supplied with hard but plastic muscles on the front and outside, with tightly-stretched tendons on the inside and at the back.*

(d) JOINT *between Forearm and Foot (wrists): These are closer together than the shoulder joints, so that the front does not appear absolutely straight.*

(e) PAWS: *Full, broad in front, and a trifle inclined outwards; compact, with well-arched toes and tough pads.*

(f) TOES: *There are five of these, though only four are in use. Dewclaws may be removed. They should be close together, with a pronounced arch; provided on top with strong nails, and underneath with tough toe-pads.*

The front leg, or arm, includes: shoulder blade, upper arm, forearm, and foot. The shoulder blades, and with them the front limbs, are connected to the trunk only by muscles and ligaments. If this connection is too loose, one speaks of loose shoulders, and if it is too tight, of pinched shoulders. Both of these conditions are disadvantageous in motion.

Ch. Tanga-Ta Piccadilly Circus; judge Grace Hirschman. Co-owners James L. (handling) and Irene M. Swyler of Virginia. Photo by Delma Hunteen.

Hindquarters—*The hindquarters viewed from behind should be of completely equal width.*

(*a*) CROUP: *Long, round, full, robustly muscled, but plastic, only slightly sinking toward the tail.*

(*b*) PELVIC BONES: *Not too short, rather strongly developed, and moderately sloping.*

(*c*) THIGH BONE: *Robust and of good length, set at right angles to the pelvic bones.*

(*d*) HIND LEGS: *Robust and well-muscled, with well-rounded buttocks.*

(*e*) KNEE JOINT: *Broad and strong.*

(*f*) CALF BONE: *In comparison with other breeds, short; it should be perpendicular to the thigh bone, and firmly muscled.*

(*g*) *The bones at the* BASE OF THE FOOT (*tarsus*) *should present a flat appearance, with a strongly prominent hock and a broad tendon of Achilles.*

(*h*) *The* CENTRAL FOOT BONES (*metatarsus*) *should be long, movable towards the calf bone, slightly bent toward the front, but perpendicular (as viewed from behind).*

(*i*) HIND PAWS: *Four compactly-closed and beautifully-arched toes, as in the case of the front paws. The whole foot should be posed equally on the ball and not merely on the toes; nails short.*

The hindquarters of the dog supply the driving power for forward motion, which is transmitted by way of the back to the front leg in the process of stepping forward. It includes the pelvic bones, the thigh, and the foot (paw and toes). The Dachshund should cover neither too much nor too little ground space, i.e., he should not have a Bulldog-like broad stance, but neither should he have a Greyhound-like narrow stance.

The FOOTWORK is mostly dependent on the build of the front legs, the back, the hind legs, and the inter-relationship of these parts.

To the extent that it is a self-propelled machine, the animal body, and therefore also the Dachshund body, is dependent on the laws of mechanics.

The more functionally a machine is built, the more it can produce and the less power it wastes. The more the mechanism is to the purpose of the Dachshund, the more plentiful and enduring is his ability to work, the less strength he uses up.

As a self-propelled machine, the Dachshund must meet, with the highest efficiency possible, the demands put to him as a many-sided hunting assistant. As a hound and search dog, he must have at his command perseverance

Ch. Bush's Big John Goodox St.; judge Thirza Hibner. Co-owners Dale and Sally Keyes of New Mexico; handler Marilyn Delk. Photo by Morry Twomey.

for running, for overcoming obstacles in the hunting terrain (rocks, thicket, swamps, deep snow, etc.), and for keeping up a certain speed in the pursuit of healthy and wounded game. As a dog trained to follow a blood trail, he must be especially capable of overcoming any difficult situation arising from the lay of the land. The best nose does not help a Dachshund if he has to leave the trail because his build is unsuitable, either too low or too heavy; if he comes to a brook, a swamp, deep foliage, or snow, he has to spend time anxiously seeking an easier access where he can move on. As a worker below the ground the mechanism of his body must be so arranged that he can squeeze himself through narrow passages, climb steps, and dig, at least in softer parts of the ground. Especially in this area a less suitable body, built for less perseverance, can be a fatal handicap.

Flexibility and agility are a prerequisite. R. Strebel rightfully said: "In evaluating the anatomical structure of the dog, the mistake is often made to take the anatomy of the horse as a basis. There is a tremendous difference! The horse always has to carry or to pull or to do both. This, then, is the reason why the horse has to be sturdy. The dog appears to be almost the opposite. The body build should be flexible, and the musculature of the

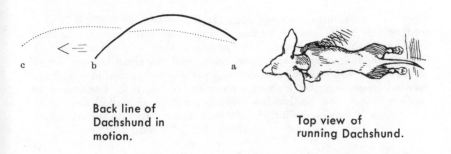

Back line of
Dachshund in
motion.

Top view of
running Dachshund.

shoulder and hip joints stretchable and pliable." In contrast it is regrettable that many judges make the mistake of giving preference to "pinched shoulders" over more mobile ones. Of course, the judge must be able to distinguish between mobile shoulders and loose shoulders.

After this preliminary consideration, let us take up the subject of the Dachshund's mechanism for motion in more detail. It can be divided into three principal parts: 1. the back, 2. the front leg, 3. the hind leg.

The back has the job of a spring. Because of the combined action of its muscles and those of the front and hind legs, the back first bends with each step and even more with each leap; then, when bounding forward, the back straightens out. Therefore, with each bound (stretching) the body is propelled forward. In reality, the forward movement actually is achieved more by pushing off with the hind legs, which follow through and then reach forward beyond the front legs. Hence the back may not be too short, in order to achieve the necessary tension. But it must not be too long either, since that would loosen the tension. One finds a slightly arched back in breeds with the most sprightly walkers. A sunken back, on the other hand, is often found in the Dachshund; this condition is completely faulty because it makes the spring-like action more difficult and leads to an early fatigue. Only an especially strong hind leg could somewhat compensate for the imperfect action of the back.

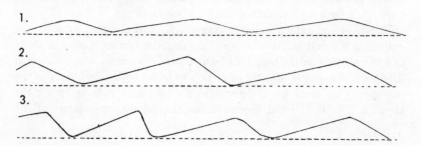

Motion-lines ot three running dogs. 1. Dachshund of medium length, medium low build, and of medium weight; well balanced coordination with good walking-mechanism; the motion is even and unhampered. 2. Dachshund of low build with long body, and therefore heavier, which forces him to leap too high in order to propel the longer and heavier body forward; assuming the walking-mechanism is good. 3. Dachshund of medium length and medium low build but poorly angulated arm, which is not able to receive the push of the hind legs evenly and without effort. Dog 1 expends least effort, dog 3 the most effort.

The front leg initially has the task of providing the body with a support after being propelled forward by the spring-like action of the back and the pushing off by the hind legs. The repeated bouncing (landing) on the ground would be painful and the pads sore and used up if the repeated impact was not softened considerably by the elasticity of the shoulders and joints of the front legs. The spring-like action, the elasticity, and the protective softening of the impact is greater, the more oblique the shoulder blades and the better the angulation of the joints of the front legs. Anyone can check the value of good angulation on his own body. The impact of jumping down from a high place to the hard ground is greatly reduced if you can angulate your joints, in other words, land in a deep knee bend. If, on the other hand, you jump with stiff knees and insufficient angulation, the impact will be too strong and not endurable for long. A steep stance and faulty angulation are therefore equivalent to a certain stiffness in the legs.

The walking-mechanism of the Dachshund. (The white lines show a schematic view.)

Illustrated here is a schematic drawing of two Dachshunds of equal size. Dog 1-2-3-4-5-, 7-8-9-10-11 is well built. He has a large obliquely set shoulder blade (1-2), a long upper arm (2-3) at right angle to it, and a well-angulated lower arm (3-4). The same holds true for the hind foot of this ideal dog. The pelvic bone (7-8) corresponding to the long, broad, and oblique shoulder blade is also long, broad and set obliquely. The large thigh bone (8-9) comes off at a right angle from the hip joint. The remaining angulation is also accordingly ample.

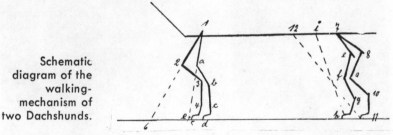

Schematic diagram of the walking-mechanism of two Dachshunds.

In contrast the dog 1-a-b-c-d-, 7-e-f-g-h demonstrates a faulty front leg and hind leg. His shoulder blade (1-a) is not set as oblique, that is, it is steeper than the shoulder blade 1-2; it is also shorter and narrower. The upper arm (a-b) is also shorter than the upper arm 2-3; it is not connected to the shoulder blade at a right angle, but by an obtuse angle. Accordingly the lower arm is in an unfavorable position. Thus the faulty, steeper line 1-a-b-c-d is also shorter than the well-angulated line 1-2-3-4-5. The same faults are apparent in the hind leg 7-e-f-g-h; it is too steep because it is poorly (obtusely) angulated. In general, as well as in individual bone structure, it is shorter than the ideal hind leg 7-11.

We previously saw that a steeper, shorter, inflexible front leg suffers from inadequate resiliency in a leap to the ground. Such legs are also incapable of taking big strides, as the figure shows. When the steep front leg 1-d takes a step forward by straightening out (1-a-e), it only moves forward by the distance d-e. In comparison when the well-angulated front leg (1-5) is extended and steps forward (1-6), it moves forward by a much greater distance!

Correspondingly, the well-angulated hind leg 7-11 pushes the body forward, when extended (walking), by the distance 7-12. The steeper and shorter hind leg (7-h) only moves across 7-i. Therefore the well-built dog saves strength and time and gains in perseverance. He also makes a more appealing sight because of his well-proportioned movements.

In evaluating the walking-mechanism, which presupposes a knowledge of the anatomical-mechanical facts we described above, mistakes are often made by judges, breeders, and fanciers. On the other hand, it is here that a competent judge is only too often unjustly reproached by ignorant exhibitors. The exhibitor sees that his dog is obviously superior to the others in shape of head, in color, tail, etc., but is put back anyway. The grave

Ch. Karlstadt's Mahareshi, Smooth Dappled Standard Dachshund; judge Dr. C. William Nixon. Owner-handler Barbara M. Murphy. Photo by Evelyn M. Shafer.

Ch. Doxlane's Chocolate Toffee, Smooth Chocolate Standard Dachshund; judge William Held. Co-owners Mrs. Grover Schiltz and Mrs. Harlene Walter of Illinois; handler Hannelore Heller. Photo by Delma Hunteen.

faults of the walking-mechanism, which were the reason for his dog being put back, he does not see at all, nor can he understand them, since he is lacking the basic knowledge of this mechanism. Everyone who is interested in the evaluation of Dachshunds is well advised to read this chapter carefully and absorb it well. We repeat, once more, in a short summary, those points which are most important: firm, medium-long, very slightly arched back section; long and full withers; strong, only slightly rounded kidney section; long, broad, oblique shoulder blades, which are connected to the body by strong, elastic, but not too long, ligaments. (Good, long shoulder blades almost meet near the top of the back); long, powerful, but not clumsy, bones of the upper arm which should be set at right angles to the shoulder blades; deeply joined, short wrists; closed, firm paws. Perfectly angulated, strong, broad hind legs. "In the low, crooked position of the legs lies the basis of the Dachshund's weakness [in comparison to the Fox Terrier]." Therefore the Dachshund should not stand too low nor too crooked, especially since the length of the back tends to increase this weakness.

Charzans' Silverplate-L (born black-and-tan is gradually changing to a silver-blue). Judge George C. Spradling. Co-owners Charles and Suzanne Spillman of New York; handler Charles Spillman. Photo by Martin Booth.

The musculature of the walking-mechanism must be hard and clear-cut. Too stout, spongy musculature, especially in the front legs, is useless. Such an overburdened shoulder makes the walk awkward and is a handicap while crawling through tight passages in dens, so much more so, since most often this condition goes together with a barrel-shaped chest.

One more item we have to note: the position of both the right and the left front leg and the right and the left hind leg relative to each other. We have already seen that the muscles which connect the shoulder blade with the body (withers and ribs) should not be too short and thick, because the shoulder is hampered in its movement (bound, or pinched, shoulder). Equally bad is the opposite, the "loose shoulder," which is the result of too long and supple muscle connections. With each step this shoulder slides up along the chest; furthermore, it deviates sideways from the body so that most often the elbows are strongly pointed outward. Thereby both elbows diverge instead of staying close together and parallel. The shoulder should have ease of movement, but only along the direction of the body,

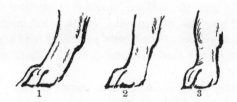

Pastern. 1. Too soft, bent backwards;
frequent fault in Dachshunds who "should
not knuckle". 2. Good pastern. 3. Too
steep which favors knuckling.

Correct stance (side).

Correct stance (rear).

Incorrect stance; cow hocks.

Incorrect stance; bow legs.

not away from it. Since the hind legs should also stand and work parallel to each other, one can talk of a parallel walking-mechanism. In contrast, faulty front legs have turned-out elbows and faulty hind legs have the so-called cow hocks, where the heels come closely together, and in bad cases even touch.

NOTE:—*Inasmuch as the Dachshund is a hunting dog, scars from honorable wounds shall not be considered a fault.*

II.—SPECIAL CHARACTERISTICS OF THE THREE COAT-VARIETIES OF DACHSHUND

The Dachshund is bred with three varieties of coat (A) Shorthaired (or Smooth); (B) Wirehaired; (C) Longhaired.

Silhouette of the three coat varieties.

All three varieties should conform to the characteristics already specified.

The longhaired and shorthaired are old, well-fixed varieties, but into the wirehaired Dachshund, the blood of other breeds has been purposely introduced; nevertheless, in breeding him, the greatest stress must be placed upon conformity to the general Dachshund type.

The following specifications are applicable separately to the three coat varieties, respectively:

(A) Shorthaired (or Smooth) Dachshund—HAIR: *Short, thick, smooth and shining; no bald patches. Special faults are: Too fine or thin hair; leathery ears, bald patches, too coarse or too thick hair in general.*

TAIL—*Gradually tapered to a point, well but not richly haired; long; sleek bristles on the underside are considered a patch of strong-growing hair, not a fault.*

A brush tail is a fault, as is also a partly- or wholly-hairless tail.

COLOR OF HAIR, NOSE AND NAILS—(*a*) ONE-COLORED DACHSHUND: *This group includes red (often called tan), red-yellow, yellow, and brindle, with or without a shading of interspersed black hairs. Nevertheless a clean color is preferable, and red is to be considered more desirable than red-yellow or yellow. Dogs strongly shaded with interspersed black hairs belong to this class, and not to the other color groups.*

Ch. Celloyd Virginia Woolf; owner Howard Atlee of New York.

Ch. Dunkeldorf Falcon's Favorite, owned by T.R. Dunk, Jr., sired over 50 champions.

A small white spot is admissible but not desirable.

NOSE AND NAILS—*Black; brown is admissible but not desirable.*

(b) TWO-COLORED DACHSHUND: *These comprise deep black, chocolate, gray (blue) and white; each with tan markings over the eyes, on the sides of the jaw and underlip, on the inner edge of the ear, front, breast, inside and behind the front legs, on the paws and around the anus, and from there to about one-third to one-half of the length of the tail on the under side. The most common two-colored Dachshund is usually called black-and-tan. A small white spot is admissible but not desirable. Absence, undue prominence or extreme lightness of tan markings is undesirable.*

NOSE AND NAILS—*In the case of black dogs, black; for chocolate, brown (the darker the better); for gray (blue) or white dogs, gray or even flesh color, but the last named color is not desirable; in the case of white dogs, black nose and nails are to be preferred.*

Ch. Torals Sweet Bramble; judge Mrs. Clifford Burian. Owner Mary Castoral of New York; handler Howard Nygood. Photo by Evelyn M. Shafer.

(c) DAPPLED DACHSHUND—*The color of the dappled Dachshund is a clear brownish or grayish color, or even a white ground, with dark irregular patches of dark-gray, brown, red-yellow or black (large areas of one color not desirable'). It is desirable that neither the light nor the dark color should predominate.*

NOSE AND NAILS—*As for One- and Two-Colored Dachshund.*

The hair should be very dense, rather short, but not too scanty or shiny (nor dull or dry); it should cover the body evenly. The ventral side often has too thin a growth of hair. According to his functions, a Dachshund coat should rather be too coarse than too fine, even if he runs the "risk" of appearing less "noble."

Ch. Westphal's Shillalah (#1 Dachshund—all coats—1970; and is way ahead for 1971); judge William Shores. Owner Peggy Westphal of New York; handler Lorraine Heichel. Photo by Earl Graham.

(B) Wirehaired Dachshund—*The general appearance is the same as that of the shorthaired, but without being long in the legs, it is permissible for the body to be somewhat higher off the ground.*

HAIR—*With the exception of jaw, eyebrows, and ears, the whole body is covered with a perfectly uniform, tight, short, thick, rough, hard coat, but with finer, shorter hairs (undercoat) everywhere distributed between the coarser hairs resembling the coat of the German spiky-haired Pointer. There should be a beard on the chin.*

The eyebrows are bushy; on the ears the hair is shorter than on the body, almost smooth, but in any case conforming to the rest of the coat. The general arrangement of the hair should be such that the wirehaired Dachshund, when seen from a distance should resemble the smooth-haired.

Any sort of soft hair in the coat is faulty, whether short or long, or wherever

Coat of soft wirehair, very faulty.

found on the body; the same is true of long, curly, or wavy hair, or hair that sticks out irregularly in all directions; a flag tail is also objectionable.

TAIL—*Robust, as thickly haired as possible, gradually coming to a point, and without a tuft.*

COLOR OF HAIR, NOSE AND NAILS—*All colors are admissible. White patches on the chest though allowable, are not desirable.*

Of all the coat varieties the wirehaired Dachshund is the most difficult to breed and therefore is the least uniform. The wirehair should completely match in bodily conformation the smooth Dachshund.

The so-called undercoat gives increased protection to the dog because of the warm air contained between the cover hair and the skin.

The wirehaired Dachshund, best fitted for practical use, must exhibit the following properties: 1. wirehair type, 2. medium length, 3. harshness of

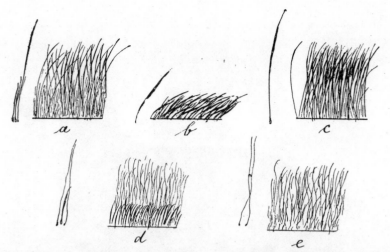

Different types of wirehair. a) Hard coverhair with soft wooly undercoat. b) Hard, short wirehair without undercoat. c) Long wirehair, fine below and thick above, forming a warm, insulating layer of air between skin and thick outer layer of hair. d) Short, hard "coverhair" with an overgrowth of soft wooly undercoat. (Faulty) e) Soft, long, wooly hair, throughout. (Very faulty)

coat, 4. close-fitting coat, 5. undercoat medium grade. The latter is often very pronounced in the winter, but only hinted at during the summer.

(C) Longhaired Dachshund—*The distinctive characteristic differentiating this coat from the short- or smooth-haired Dachshund is alone the rather long silky hair.*

HAIR—*The soft sleek, glistening, often slightly-wavy hair should be longer under the neck, on the underside of the body, and especially on the ears and behind the legs, becoming there a pronounced feather; the hair should attain its greatest length on the underside of the tail. The hair should fall beyond the lower edge of the ear. Short hair on the ear, so-called "leather" ears, is not desirable. Too luxurious a coat causes the longhaired Dachshund to seem coarse, and masks the type.*

The coat should remind one of the Irish Setter, and should give the dog an elegant appearance. Too thick hair on the paws, so-called "mops," is inelegant, and renders the animal unfit for use. It is faulty for the dog to have equally long hair over all the body, if the coat is too curly, or too scrubby, or if a flag tail or overhanging hair on the ear is lacking, or if there is a very pronounced parting on the back, or a vigorous growth between the toes.

TAIL—*Carried gracefully in prolongation of the spine; the hair attains here its greatest length and forms a veritable flag.*

101

Ch. Robdachs Dominent Star; co-owners Sanford L. and Patricia A. Roberts of California. Photo by Tausken.

COLOR OF HAIR, NOSE AND NAILS—*Exactly as for the smooth-haired Dachshund, except that the red-with-black (heavily sabled) color is permissible and is formally classed as a red.*

In a shorn condition, the longhaired Dachshund should look exactly like the smooth. When one crosses smooth Dachshunds with longhaired Dachshunds, smooths almost always result. (*See Ch. III. Genetics*). However, the smooth, in most cases, appears to profit by a denser, longer coat in place of the all too fine smooth coat. The addition of longhair blood is well suited for the improvement of a too fine or "over-refined" smooth coat, with a tendency to baldness on the ears and on the tail. Later infusion of wirehair blood frequently brought about most attractive and good wirehair coat which was well transmitted to later generations. These experiments should be continued by the wirehair Dachshund people, if only for scientific and practical reasons. The hesitation of such ventures rests only with lack of experience.

The basic form of dog hair is a tight, coarse type of hair (*Stockhaar* or "stockhair"), as seen in the wild dog; this then, is and remains the best hair. The smooth hair of the domesticated dog represents a stunting of this hair, a decline in its length and thickness. Longhair is only a refinement of stockhair, an elongation at the expense of the strength of the single hair. Wirehair is a loosening up of the stockhair, almost like a swelling up of the single hair. In this way the hair lengthens and thickens, so much so, that the hairs push each other apart. The best smooth coat was often obtained by crossings with coarse longhair. The smooth hair turned out to be longer and denser. Less advantageous was the pairing of wirehair with smooth. The most unhappy outcome resulted from attempts to improve the wirehair through crosses with fine smooth stock. Unfortunately the smooth Dachshund shown in dog shows has hair which is most often too soft; most of the time the shortness of hair only simulates harshness.

Concerning the working-type Dachshunds one may rightly ask: "Which coat is preferable in practice ?" Naturally each fancier sings his special song, and we grant it to him. Anyone who, like Dr. Engelmann, keeps all three coat varieties, does not need to take sides. The advantages and disadvantages are pretty well balanced. The highly bred smooth Dachshund, who frequently has too short and too fine a coat on the ears and tail, has a tendency to become easily chilled. However, if he has a lot of hunting fever, then he can endure even rough weather. The coarse-haired dog, though, is always better, even if he appears less "refined" to the layman. The smooth has the

Family of Winners at Dachshund Club of California, 1970 Show: center, Best of Breed, Ch. Wayt-A-While Parade, owner Ethel Bigler of California; left, Best of Opposite Sex to Best of Breed, "Wayt's" daughter, Ch. Von Relgib's Red Witch, co-owners Herbert and Elaine Holtzman of California; and right, Best Puppy in Sweepstakes, Winner Dog, and Best of Winners, Von Relgib's Grand Marshal, co-owners the Holtzmans. Photo by Alfred Stillman.

advantage of drying fast and snow, ice, and dirt do not stick to him. The long-haired can hunt for hours in the rain without ever getting a single drop of water on his skin. He is quite indifferent to cold. One has to admit, though, that he dries slower. Snow and ice often hang in annoying clumps all over his body. Snow clots are especially troublesome between his toes, so that many times the dog cannot move but has to stop to nibble off the little lumps of ice. For this reason cutting short the hair on the feet and especially the toes in the winter-time is a practical maneuver. Besides that, the longhaired does not require any grooming, contrary to general opinion. He is equally resistant to inclement weather as is the wirehaired. At first glance, the latter gives the impression that he is superior to the other in this respect. But this statement can be granted only conditionally. Wirehairs with an ideal coat are infinitely rare—short, very coarse, tight, and close-fitting wire hair sheds the water—but with the average wirehair of today this is not the case. Instead it soaks up the water and then takes a longer time to dry out. Furthermore, even in tolerably good wirehair, numerous annoying ice and

Ch. Verdon's Vici M; judge John P. Murphy. Co-owners Tom and Kathryn (at left) Curtis of Ohio; handler Katherine Posch Wade. Photo by D. Garverick, C.P.P.

Emblem of the National Miniature Dachshund Club. Photo by William Brown.

snow clumps tend to form, often more so than in the longhaired. The not really harsh wirehaired Dachshund is the one most likely to need grooming, since he must be plucked frequently and his hair must always be kept short. Because of the earlier infusion of the blood of German Pinschers and English wirehair Terriers (Dandie Dinmont Terriers), the wirehaired Dachshunds of today still have a good dose of the best characteristics of these active, robust breeds, which retarded the effects of overbreeding for a long time.

Miniature Dachshunds—

Miniature Dachshunds are bred in all three coats. Within the limits imposed, symmetrical adherence to the general Dachshund conformation, combined with smallness, and mental and physical vitality, should be the outstanding characteristics of Miniature Dachshunds. They have not been given separate classification but are a division of the Open Class for "under ten pounds and twelve months old or over."

Ch. Patchwork Hill Calliope (top winning Longhaired Miniature Dachshund of all time); judge Haywood Hartley. Owner Peggy Westphal of New York; handler Howard Nygood. Photo by William P. Gilbert.

Dachs-Haven's Cleopatra MS, at fourteen months of age. Judge Bernard Ziessow. Co-owned by Tom (handling) and Kathryn Curtis of Ohio.

The large number of non-hunters among Dachshund fanciers created many weight classes for sporting and show purposes; it would go too far if we were to concern ourselves with them here.

In hunting practice two SIZES of Dachshunds are needed: one size which can work comfortably in fox burrows, as well as in mother-dens and escape holes; and a second size for use in rabbit warrens and other tight hiding places of martens, ferrets, fox cubs, etc. The larger type weighs from 11 to $16\frac{1}{2}$ lbs. (5-7$\frac{1}{2}$ Kg.) and the chest circumference should have a maximum of $16\frac{1}{2}''$ (42 cm.). Numerous experiences have taught that bigger dogs often cannot work their way through the dens. The second working type (the Rabbit Dachshund) should weigh $4\frac{1}{4}$ lbs. (2 Kg.) or, more accurately, should have a chest circumference which should not exceed $9\frac{1}{2}''$ (24 cm.). Otherwise, in most rabbit warrens, he will be very cramped. At this time though, one has to accept Rabbit Dachshunds with $11''$ (28 cm.) chest circumference, since this type still has to be made to breed small and true.

Ch. Lawndalis Shoo Shoo pictured at only seven months old; judge Mrs. Philip (Eleanor) Bishop. Owner Peggy Westphal of New York; handler Lorraine Heichel. Photo by Morry Twomey.

At present a peculiar uncertainty prevails in wide circles about the procedure needed to breed for a type of Dachshund capable of hunting rabbits, ferrets, etc. below the ground—the Rabbit Dachshund. It is true that different breeds have been used for crosses, but the results were not encouraging. One quickly came back to pure Dachshund blood. The much too large Miniature Dachshunds, or so-called Miniature Dachshunds, who weigh from $8\frac{3}{4}$ lbs. to 11 lbs. (4 Kg. to 5 Kg.), are like giants in comparison to Rabbit Dachshunds.

A good and useful Rabbit Dachshund should weigh from $4\frac{1}{2}$ lbs. to $5\frac{1}{2}$ lbs. (2 Kg. to $2\frac{1}{2}$ Kg.), just about half as much as the "Miniature."

The younger ones among us may live to see the day when agreement is reached on more natural measures contingent upon hunting purposes:

lbs.	Kg.	
$4\frac{1}{2}$ - $6\frac{1}{2}$	2 - 3	Rabbit Dachshund
$7\frac{3}{4}$ - 11	$3\frac{1}{2}$ - 5	Light Dachshund
12 - $16\frac{1}{2}$	$5\frac{1}{2}$ - $7\frac{1}{2}$	Heavy Dachshund
above $17\frac{1}{2}$	above 8	Overweight (faulty size)

Because their size was set with a definite purpose in mind, and because

Ch. Patchwork Johnny Come Lately; owner Patricia Beresford Fowler of Virginia. Photo by William P. Gilbert.

American and Canadian Champion Tori Russet Princess; owner Thomas J. Rice of New York. Photo by Tausken.

they have primarily a practical value, every hunter can work with these figures.

In the den of a mother vixen these smallest of the Miniature Dachshunds proved themselves excellently. They have also earned top prizes in field trials on fox and badger dens. In addition, these Rabbit Dachshunds have shown themselves to be capable above the ground. In any case, a too large Dachshund cannot perform any better than a 16½ lb. dog; this fact can be proven again and again by the actual experience of the hunt, as well as in field trials. Further weight classifications are of no practical value. Dachshunds weighing more than 16½ lbs. (7½ Kg.) appear unpleasantly big, and, as mentioned before, often enough cannot work their way through a difficult fox den. Therefore any weight above 16½ lbs. should be considered as faulty, because this weight would imply a chest circumference of more than 16½" (42 cm.), as long as the dog is not too narrow chested for its size. In measuring the size of working dogs one has to be completely objective and be guided only by the potentiality for work. The chest circumference of the badger fluctuates between 15"-15¾" (38-40 cm.); but is is very rare that one reaches 15¾". The fox also, like all the other cave-dwellers, has a small chest circumference: 12¾"-14¼" (32-36 cm.), seldom 15"-15¾" (38-40 cm.). The

Ch. Pegremes Brigette L., judge Rose Heying. Owner-handler Peter G. Monks of Virginia. Photo by Bridges Photos.

rabbit has a medium chest circumference of $9\frac{3}{4}''$ (25 cm.). For obvious reasons one cannot breed earth-going dogs more voluminous than the animals they have to pursue everywhere below the earth! Just as a chimney sweep must not be fatter than the chimney!

Color does not really matter when working the dens; only the worst Sunday hunter could confuse the Dachshund with a fox or a badger. The red color, while probably one of the most attractive, is also quite unsuitable. Particularly while searching through low thickets and pursuing game, especially during drives, the red and the stag color often has been fatal for their bearers. Even the calmest marksman can find himself in the embarrassing situation of grasping his gun a little firmer when the red Dachshund chases through the red bushes in their autumn colors and the yellow grass, brush, or heather. Almost without exception, it is Dachshunds with red coats who are "bagged." On a drive in 1905, a sure marksman took aim at the red longhaired "Vossa v. Sonnenstein," who was driving through pole timber. The bitch was immediately leashed! Two red Dachshunds were shot while blocking (pursuing game), one by his owner! Impractical during such drives are also indistinguishably dappled dogs. Strangely enough, it is the bright white dappled and the blotched dappled dogs, who at most could only once, and then for but a moment, be mistaken for a colorful cat, who are bred the least. The black-and-tan Dachshund is most protected by its color.

III.—GENERAL FAULTS

Serious Faults—*Over- or undershot jaws, knuckling over, very loose shoulders.*

Secondary Faults—*A weak, long-legged, or dragging figure, body hanging between the shoulders; sluggish, clumsy, or waddling gait; toes turned inwards or too obliquely outwards; splayed paws, sunken back, roach (or carp) back; croup*

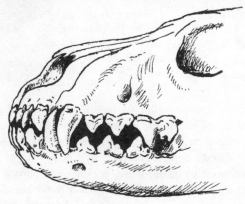

Pincer teeth.

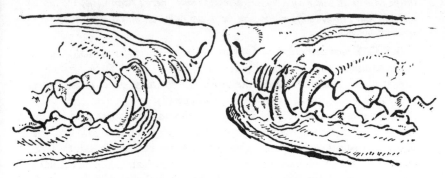

Overshot bite.   Undershot bite.

Too low in front, too high in back; straight hind legs (as in this case) are a frequent cause of this condition. Head is too short and blunt. Tail is too thick and long. Chest is too round. Front paws are set too far forward (knuckling backward).

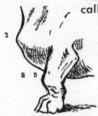

(1-2) So-called "chicken breast" (3) Knuckling wrist (falsely called knee).

Fore arm set too far in front; the front legs should cover the lowest point of the chest (a).

higher than withers; short-ribbed or too-weak chest; excessively drawn-up flanks like those of a Greyhound; narrow, poorly-muscled hindquarters; weak loins; bad angulation in front or hindquarters; cow hocks; bowed legs; wall eyes, except for dappled dogs; a bad coat.

Minor Faults—Ears wrongly set, sticking out, narrow or folded; too marked a stop; too pointed or weak a jaw; pincer teeth; too wide or too short a head; goggle eyes, wall eyes in the case of dappled dogs; insufficiently dark eyes in the case of all other coat-colors; dewlaps; short neck; swan neck; too fine or too thin hair; absence of, or too profuse to too light tan markings in the case of two-colored dogs.

A.K.C. Disqualification: Lack of two normal testicles normally located in the scrotum.

A medium height is always desirable, the so-called good *Bodenabstand* ("distance from ground to lowest point of chest").

Unsuitable size and weight. No earthdog should weigh more than $16\frac{1}{2}$ lbs. ($7\frac{1}{2}$ Kg.); the chest circumference should always remain less than 17" (43 cm.). Instead of the spongy girth, of an excess ballast of meat, skin, fat, and bones, one should strive for solid compact material. Compare the hard-as-nails bones of the wild rabbit with the much thicker and looser bone structure of the domestic rabbit; compare the hard slender bones of the wild boar with the soft, spongy, broad bones of the domestic pig. Which kind of bone structure is more desirable for the working dog is not difficult to guess.

Too long, too weak, too strongly curved or sunken back (roach back and sway back). One differentiates in the sunken back between the sway back, in which the lowest part of the back lies between the withers and the croup, and the sloping back, in which the croup stands higher than the withers.

Ugly and faulty is a tail which is set too high, too strongly bent, or hooklike (the so-called post-horn), as well as a tail which is too thick, coarse, too thin, too long, or poorly coated (rat's tail).

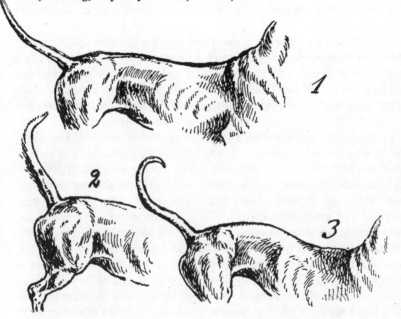

Carriage of the tail. 1. Well-carried tail; 2. Steeply carried bushy tail; 3. Roach back and strongly curved tail.

Coarse coats should not be counted as faulty.

Faults in structure are always more serious than those of color. First the house then the painting.

Knuckling over is a frequent fault in Dachshunds. Opinions are divided as to the causes. The Delegate Commission published the Breed Characteristics, which several clubs accepted. The following sentences were included: "The biggest fault in evaluating Dachshunds is not to have recognized the cause of knuckling; it is to be sought merely in bad shoulder development and its position. Steep, narrow, short shoulders are always connected with a steep, short upper arm, poorly developed breastbone and pointed chest (chicken breast). The awkward and steep shoulder angle should give rise, analogously, to an acute and flexible angle at the elbow. However, this is not the case; instead the short upper arm is bent out and the forearm is pushed forward and inward. Thereby the center of gravity is moved too far forward and support of the body only becomes possible by a bending forward of the wrists and the pastern (so-called knuckling or toppling over). Broad, long and oblique shoulders guarantee, despite hardships, a good posture to a ripe old age; while narrow, short and steep shoulders usually necessitate a turning out of the upper arm, loose ligaments and always poor support of the body." To this statement R. Strebel comments:

"This version is incorrect, because I have seen Dachshunds with very long shoulders with excellent angulation at the upper arms, who knuckled; and vice versa, dogs with very steep shoulders and short upper arms, who did not knuckle. . . . Loose shoulders, set too far to the front, steep and short upper arms, and turned out feet are the cause of knuckling. But that does not mean that all these conditions have to occur at the same time."

Every observer of Dachshunds will know of cases of one-sided knuckling. In one such one-sided knuckler observed for several years and in all sorts of positions, both shoulder blades were placed equally well, the upper arms had excellent angulation, and the stance of the forearms also was absolutely unobjectionable. After the dog's death, the bones of the forearms were prepared and measured carefully. There was no difference between the right and the left side, but nevertheless the dog had knuckled on one side. The only apparent reason was that when the dog was alive the toes of the knuckling foot were pointed outward relative to the other foot which pointed more to the front. The knuckling foot was turned too far on its length axis, so much so, that the toes pointed too far to the side and therefore touched the ground further back than those of the normal foot. In other words, in relation to the elbow, the toes were too far back.

The weight of the body is supported wrongly and is pushed forward; therefore the joint at the base of the foot has to give and knuckles over. Consequently it is the crooked position that seems to be the cause in most cases. Thus the fact can be explained that in straight-legged breeds, dogs with the steepest stance and loose shoulders almost never knuckle over, not even when they become weak through sickness or old age. On the other hand, one can observe often enough that otherwise surefooted Dachshunds knuckle over occasionally, as a result of a false step where the paw comes too far out and back (the so-called occasional knuckler). It would be wrong to classify these dogs as knucklers. You can demonstrate to yourself on your own body the main cause of knuckling: stand correctly; then while keeping

114

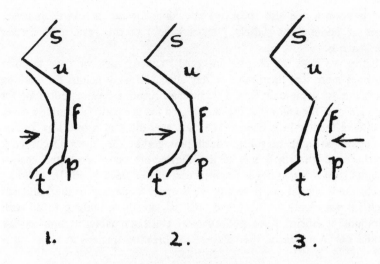

Front legs of three Dachshunds.

your heels firmly in their proper place, turn the feet as far out as possible, so that they form almost a straight line across; you will notice that your knees will have to bend forward. One can make similar observations on people with knock-knees and outwardly pointed flat feet.

In the accompanying figure of three different Dachshunds, the posture is completely different, even though their size and the angulation of the shoulder and upper arm is the same. Dog 1 stands firm and correct. Dog 2 achieves a "firm stance," the inability to knuckle, because of the double-joint effect (knuckling backward). Dog 3 displays just the opposite: the forearm (f) is joined to the upper arm (u) toward the front instead of being straight or slightly bent backward; while the forearm (f), connecting with the pastern (p), bends backward, in contrast to dogs 1 and 2. In other words: upper arm, forearm, and pastern form a correctly backward-curved line in dog 1, and a too strongly backward-curved line in dog 2 (double-jointedness or "knuckling backward"), and a faulty line which is curved forward (causing the dog to knuckle over) in dog 3.

This double-jointedness toward the back (2) causes an over-exertion of the ligaments of the joints in fast running or when leaping up which eventually may lead to a "pushed through pastern." Knuckling over is naturally not possible here. The one fault excludes the other. This double-jointedness toward the back is often found in Dachshunds whose "firm" stance (toward the front) is undeservedly praised too much. Apart from knuckling forward and backward, one also speaks of knuckling toward the inside in severe cases of fiddle front (falsely, "knock-knee") of the pastern in narrow Dachshunds.

Before we close the chapter on breed characteristics, we have to point out once more that their value is very small, in many points, for working Dachshunds. Some only have a traditional, customary value, but none for performance. We know that the long-legged fox is equally as nimble a cave-dweller as the low-built badger. We know that the long-legged Fox Terrier is equally as agile in subterranean passages as the lower Dachshund. Furthermore, the small ears of the Terrier are better protected against assaults than the traditional dropped ears of the Dachshund. In addition, Dachshunds should not have any white spots, according to the standard; such rules are only arbitrary and artificial, and have nothing to do with questions of efficiency for performance. Understandably, as hunters, we should not overestimate the value of the breed characteristics. The main

Faulty: Chicken breast, sunken back, bad angulation of hind leg.

importance should always be attached to the natural hunting tendencies and their inheritance. The purest bred and most efficient structure will not be useful if the will to work is not strong enough. In choosing breeding stock we always have to keep this fact in mind.

Here, now, is the place to add a few words about the too often misunderstood term of "nobility." "Nobility" is seen in the interplay of spirit and

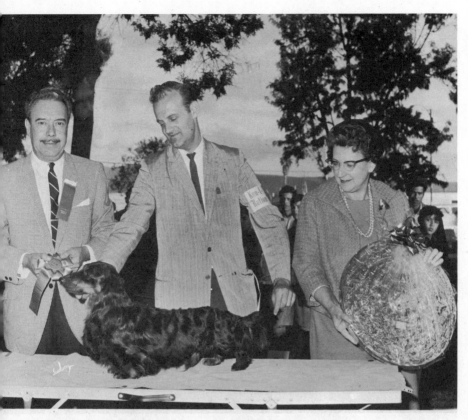

American and Mexican Champion Sweethaven Antonio L., shown winning Hound Group in Mexico under judge Sr. Ibarra. Owned by Barbara J. Nichols of California; handler Orville Evenson. Photo by Ludwig.

body. In the build it is particularly the proportions with which the figure achieves its highest perfection. This perfection reveals at first glance vigor, agility, health, and vitality. "Nobility" means a perfect balance of the individual parts of the body to each other, as well as a special balance between proportions and performance. Like a highly developed, perfected machine achieves the highest output with the least effort, so also, should the purebred dog reach a maximum of achievement by means of his noble and efficient structure with a minimum effort. In contrast to the foregoing there is overbreeding and exaggeration of some isolated, overrated points of the breed, at the expense of type and, therefore, performance. Overbreeding leads to a caricature, nobility to proportionality. "Nobility" means restraint in everything that is superfluous, overloaded bones and muscles, a chiseling away of all ballast; it means clear-cut, taut musculature; steely, not broad bones; effortless motion, which assures untiring perseverance; it confers fire and thoroughbred expression. Thoroughbred expression is something spiritual, difficult to describe, which, so to speak, emanates from perfected proportions: the sum total of all the carefully synchronized characteristics of the body and of the spirit. The most perfectly formed dog lacks nobility, if he is apathetic and languid in his spirit. The nobility of the purebred animal cannot be noticed by merely observing his conformation. It must radiate from the bearer not only at rest but also in the midst of the activities of daily life, especially in the fulfilment of his life purpose typical of his breed.

HUNTING CHARACTERISTICS

Hunting characteristics are treated most often unfairly in the breed standard for the Dachshund. The hunt created the Dachshund; only while

Ch. De Sangpur Footloose; judge Roger Van, owner Peggy Westphal of New York; handler Howard Nygood. Photo by Evelyn M. Shafer.

Ch. Villanol's Vanguard; judge Mrs. Frances C. Heaslıp, owner Jean M. Carvill of New York; handler Gordon Carvill. Photo by Wm. P. Gilbert.

hunting does he show himself completely; the hunt must also preserve him. Otherwise he would sink to a level of practical insignificance, he would become a toy and a commodity.

A Dachshund without vigorous hunting attributes simply is no Dachshund, because he lacks that which justifies the name of the breed. A Dachshund with a lukewarm or even cold hunting spirit is like a knife without a blade, a cartridge without powder.

The breed characteristics must demand of the Dachshund, along with correct size, the maximum of vigor, agility, perseverance, resistance, and aggressiveness. For these traits, together with a sureness in tracking, a strong will, and a certain independence of spirit form the essence of the Dachshund character.

The most distinctive breed characteristic of the Dachshund must be the inborn aggressiveness against game. An aggressiveness which grants no peace until the adversary is destroyed either through the dog's own efforts or with the help of the hunter. This "killer instinct" fosters perseverance and keenness. Without doubt, this spirit is already much weakened through the greatest curse which so heavily weights on the Dachshund, the keeping of kennels and mass breeding for untold generations.

Far more Dachshunds are bred than can be used for work. It is a basic biological law that organs which are not exercised become weaker; and that is what is happening gradually in the Dachshund to the passion which is directed against game; therefore we have an increasing number of duds among Dachshunds. There is a "school of apologists" which holds that each Dachshund has the stuff that makes him a keen and useful dog for hunting below ground, if only he would be worked in this capacity. This statement is correct only to a limited degree. One type of Dachshund, from his earliest youth and almost without any guidance, turns out to be a little devil in the field; another type of Dachshund must be trained laboriously with much patience over a period of two or three years and then turns out to be only partially useful; and a third type never learns! Only the first type has what it takes and what one calls the inborn breed characteristics of the Dachshund; the second type has only moderate ability, similar to any big pet dog who can, with effort, be made into a useful dog for entering dens.

Ch. Dunkeldorf Sunlich, judge Herman Cox. Co-owners Ann and Sid Sims of Texas, handler Roy Murray. Photo by Morry Twomey.

Ch. Wyndsonge Magnet Wyr v. Wanner. Judge Thomas R. Dunk. Owner-handler George Wanner of New Jersey. Photo by Wm. P. Gilbert.

The third type for hunting purposes is a nonentity, as one can find only too often among Dachshunds. The breed standard has to see to it that, beyond the outward appearance, the attractive character of the breed is preserved—in fact, that it remains the most distinctive trait of the breed. Today though, conditions are such that only some bloodlines in the large family of Dachshunds preserve a strong aggressiveness against game; other bloodlines behave almost indifferent; and still others fear the fox more than any other breed of dogs. By crossing these different bloodlines the sharp divisions between their hunting behavior frequently has become blurred.

Next to the inborn aggressiveness against game, which almost always goes together with a precociousness of the hunting spirit, the standard must require that the Dachshund continue to be a small but excellent tracking dog. Third, the Dachshund should have the ability to give pursuit in a small hunting district (blocking action) as well as for search in low thickets. Here then, the Dachshund should be able to replace the Dachsbracke, the Swiss Niederlaufhund, and the Basset Hound; he has to hunt loudly, not lose the trail, nor be easily deterred. It goes without saying that a breed of hunting dogs has to be capable to work in any kind of weather and is not shy of water.

A Dachshund also should be easily trained, as much as it makes sense for his size and build. It is an old fairy tale that Dachshunds fail in training.

Ch. Muriel's Lady Marine M. ("Cuddles"); judge Virgil Johnson. Co-owners Norman Walley of Ohio and Muriel Newhauser of California; handler Norman Walley. Photo by Norton of Kent.

Best Brace in Show won by Barqua's Paisley Print L. and Barqua's Ditto V. Paisley L. under judge Allan Cartwright. This mother and daughter are co-owned by David R. and Mary Q. Bartlett of Nebraska; and were handled by Ann White. Photo by Bill Francis.

We saw Dachshunds, mostly wirehaired, who strangled the fox inside the den, who lay in front of the badger for endless hours, who did not fail on the blood trail, who were good gun dogs, who retrieved the duck from the water and the pheasant from the potato field, who obediently came back on recall and lied down on signal. It is not the fault of the breed, therefore, when we have so terribly many failing, or only one-sided Dachshunds. It is because of the insufficient selection of breeding stock, because of the indolence or incompetence of the handlers, and simply because of human inadequacies in general. How much wealth is squandered uselessly, and how often club interests take priority over the promotion of the beauty and the value of Dachshunds, their proficiency and versatility!

Chapter III
Genetics:
Descent and Heredity

HISTORICAL BACKGROUND

Today the term "genetics" is familiar to almost everybody. It stands for concepts of heredity and variation. Every breeder of dogs is aware of, and strives for, the desirable qualities and traits in his kennel. Yet he is also conscious that breeding for a specific feature has many pitfalls and may involve a determined breeding program, much patience, and may last for several generations of dogs.

It is known that a dog born with a hereditary deafness can be the parent

Three generations of longhaired Miniature Dachshunds: On the outside are four months old grandchildren Tori-Jarice's Wee Banacek ML and Tori-Jarice's Wee Babette ML; on the left is Jarice's Avalon Tabatha, the granddam; on the right is the dam, Jarice's Avalon Wee Patrice ML. Owner is Hilda B. Rice of New York. Photo by Salvatore J. Miceli.

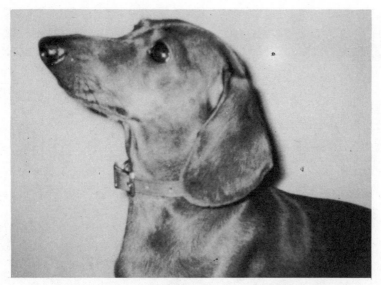
Double D Lené Katrina; owner Vera De Beck of Maine.

of puppies with normal hearing, when mated with a line carrying only normal hearing. When these puppies grow up and are allowed to mate together their offspring will produce some cases of deafness. The ratio will be one deaf puppy to three with normal hearing. On the other hand, if two deaf dogs are mated together, they will produce only deaf dogs.

Not every case is so clear-cut, nor are the causes of all types of deafness so simple. Genetics has become an important branch of biology. Research in many fields goes on continuously to determine new laws of nature, or else to improve manifold traits of numerous species.

The practice of this science is comparatively new. Better yet, let us say: the conscious formulation of its laws and the determined experimentation are comparatively recent. Selective breeding, however, has been practiced for many thousands of years. Without any knowledge of genetics—because it was not yet so formulated or in existence—Darwin proposed the origin of species in his book on evolutionary theory.

Presently there are several schools of thought on the origins of dogs.[1] One belief is that all dogs evolved from *Miacis,* a tree dweller who lived during the Eocene period some 50 million years ago. His descendants branched out into three further orders: the *procyonines,* or raccoons; the *ursines,* or bears; and the *canines.* During the Pleistocene epoch, starting about 1,000,000 years ago, the canines branched into wolves, jackals, and foxes. From this point, the schools of thoughts are divided. Some people

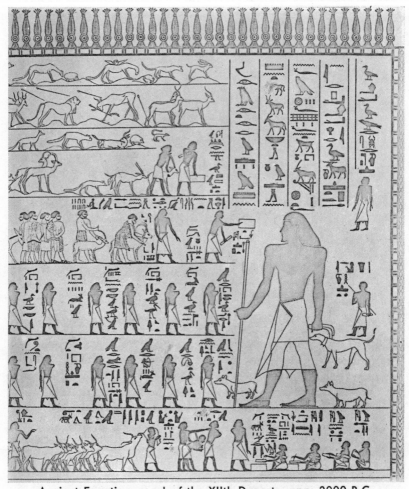

Ancient Egyptian mural of the XIIth Dynasty, app. 2000 B.C.

believe that all dogs descended most recently from the wolves. Another school had as its spokesman Prof. Konrad Lorenz[2], a noted German scientist. He advocated that some of the smaller breeds, like Dachshunds, had evolved from the jackals. Because of the differences in vocalization between jackals and dogs, Dr. Lorenz has since changed his point of view. The evidence of dogs and jackals having different numbers of chromosomes, as cited by R. Mathey[3], further negates the possibility of jackals as being ancestral to dogs.

The question which is asked most frequently is: "Did the dog, once a wild animal, choose to become a camp follower, or did man of the Mesolithic Age (Middle Stone Age) domesticate the dog as a source of food like pigs and sheep; or did prehistoric man like to keep a dog near him as a companion and partner on his inevitable hunting trips?"

From the Mesolithic, it seems dogs were protected by men. Prof. Öjvind Winge wrote on this subject[4]: "As the result of man's deliberate preservation of all newly emerged, inherited characters, the dog has become the most varied species on earth."

At the time of the height of the ancient Egyptian culture, many different breeds of dogs existed and their characteristics were recorded in the pictures of that time.

It is by now a well-known fact that the ancient Egyptians used large hounds for the pursuit of big game. But it is not as widely known that during the XIIth Dynasty, about 2000 B.C., small dogs were used to track and trail game in low bushes and underbrush. On the murals in the tomb of Khnum-Hetep (sometimes also called Chnemhôtep) we find such a hunting scene. It portrays not only a hunting scene but also the great Administrator of the Eastern Desert and Ha-prince of Menat-Khufu (Middle Egypt) accompanied by his three favorite dogs. One of them was a definite Greyhound type, but of the earless variety which is probably extinct today. The other two, a male and a female, were obviously a Dachshund-type.

The possibility[5] of a Near East origin of the Dachshund[5] as indicated by the drawings on the walls of ancient Egyptian tombs is an interesting one, although it is not necessarily accepted by either the American Kennel Club or the breed's parent club, the Dachshund Club of America. The preponderance of opinion in the D.C.A. is that the Dachshund is of German origin and was used for hunting badgers and small game by foresters and game hunters in that country. Dr. Max Hilzheimer stated that he found Dachshund skeletons with remains dating back to the Roman occupation of Germany. He had examined a large number of domestic animals of that time and found remains of Dachshunds among them. Because of his findings he believed Dachshunds must have been bred there first as no reference to them were known from other localities.[6]

Let us look at the little dappled Dachshund bitch in detail.[7]

And for easy comparison of the ancient Egyptian type with a present-day dappled Dachshund there is the picture of Ebbo von der Golg (breeder: Hans Jürgen Mayer; owner: Dr. Frederick Proewig, Wantaugh, L.I., N.Y.). The build, coat, size, color, shape of head and tail are all strikingly similar in both Dachshunds. But the obvious difference, immediately noticeable, is the position of the ears. Of course, it is well known that in ancient Egypt surgery was an art; it would have been easy for the Egyptians to crop the puppies' ears, as is done with many "modern" breeds. But we also know breeds, like the Basenji from Central Africa, with naturally erect ears. It could have been possible, also, for the ancient Dachshund-type to have had naturally erect ears. Whether natural or artificial, however, does not make any difference from the viewpoint of silhouette. We will discuss the genetic possibility a little later in this chapter.

MENDELIAN LAWS

To understand the terminology better, let us start with a short history of Gregor Johann Mendel, the father of genetics. Johann was born in 1822 in Heinzensdorf, a village in Silesia, of German parents. When he was 21 years old, he entered the Augustinian Monastery in Brünn, Moravia, as a novice; at that time he took on the name Gregor and thereafter was known by all three names. In his room and in the garden of the monastery Gregor Johann Mendel conducted his now world-famous experiments and elaborate

Modern American Dachshund, Ebbo von der Golg, owner Dr. Frederick Proewig of New York.

Closeup detail of ancient Egyptian bitch.

hybridization programs. He worked with many species, among them: bees, columbines, snapdragons, slipperworts, sedge, pumpkins, hawkweed, vetch, four-o'clocks, beans, cinquefoil, mullein, violets, maize (which has nowadays become a favorite for genetic experimentations), and his most famous, garden peas. He crossed them and then crossed the offspring of succeeding generations again and again. Long before he was elected prelate, Mendel had started his unique approach of quantitative research, essentially his statistical approach. These experiments led to what is now known as the *Mendelian Laws.*

Gregor Mendel kept a minute account of all his studies. So convenient were his notations that we today still keep the terminology Mendel used in his experiments, even though the importance of his work was not immediately nor universally recognized. Here they are:

P = for the parent generation
F_1 = for the first (filial) generation
F_2 = offspring of the F_1 generation
F_3 = progeny of crosses of the previous generation
etc., etc.

Gregor Mendel found that some of the genes (called "factors" by Mendel) carried *dominant* traits and some genes carried *recessive* traits, which might not be detected until later generations.

For an example, let us take the deaf dogs[8] again:

P = Normal x Deaf	P = Deaf x Deaf
F_1 = Normal x Normal	F_1 = *all* Deaf

F_2 = Ratio: 3 Normal to 1 Deaf

This can also be explained more visually. One has to remember that genes come in pairs (one gene from the father and one gene from the mother). It is also customary to denote the *dominant* gene by a capital letter and the *recessive* gene by the corresponding small letter.

$$D = \text{Normal Hearing}; \; d = \text{Deafness}$$

P = DD x dd
F_1 = all: Dd (Normal, as D is dominant)
F_2 = Ratio: DD, Dd, Dd, dd
P = dd x dd
F_1 = *all:* dd (deaf)

F_1 = Dd   x   Dd

F_2 = DD   Dd   dD   dd

Previously it was explained that *DD* were dominant genes and *dd* recessive genes. The combination of *Dd* will show the dominant trait. Any of these three combinations of genes is called an allele. These examples, of course, are straight forward and to the point. Not everything is as simple as

A Trio of Generations: three Longhaired Miniatures. Left, black-and-tan granddaughter, Tori-Jarice's Wee Chandra ML; front, daughter, Jarice's Avalon Wee Patrice ML; right, mother, Jarice's Avalon Tabatha ML. They are owned by a trio of breeders: Hilda, Tom and Jeanne Rice of New York.

Ch. Di-Mar's Wee Shouma; breeder-owner Mrs. Sarah Diamond of Quebec,
Canada. Photo by DNH Photographics Ltd.

this. For instance some genes show an *incomplete dominance*, or dominance
may be dependent on a certain multiple gene combination.

A mature germ cell (the male's spermatozoon or the female's ovum, or
egg) is often called a *gamete*. When the male and female gametes combine,
they become a fertilized egg, or *zygote*. When the combined genes are the
same, as in the case of *DD*'s and *dd*'s, then they are called *homozygous*,
either for the dominant or for the recessive traits. Consequently, the *Dd*'s
are called a *heterozygous* gene pair.

With this knowledge we can now identify a *phenotype* and a *genotype*.
When the traits are obvious to us (such as with dogs with normal hearing
versus those who are deaf) we speak of phenotypes. When the actual gene
combinations rather than the traits they produce are discussed (as we just
did when we explained the DD, Dd or dd), we are speaking of genotypes.

PRACTICAL APPLICATIONS

There are a few more frequently used terms which need explanation for
the dog breeder. First of all there are two important methods of propagation.

In nature, the primary type is *natural selection*, whereas the conscientious breeder who carefully considers the matings of his dogs is using *artificial selection*, or *selected breeding*. As a matter of fact the careful kennel owner will be most concerned about the stock he breeds with; therefore he is most interested in genotype as a basis for choosing desirable mating partners. This type of breeding is called *progeny selection*.

Often this type of selection turns out to be *inbreeding*. In this procedure two closely related animals are mated. Depending on the degree, this can range from brother-sister to close or distant cousins. It is obvious that in this case any hidden trait (such as *d*) is quickly brought to light by rapidly making the offspring more homozygous. At the same time it increases the probability of *DD*'s. In this manner a purer strain is more quickly established.

It has often been observed that too much inbreeding may not be desirable in the long run. Therefore *outcrossing* with another line may give good results. By introducing a completely different, but also inbred, stock, we get what is known to geneticists as *heterosis*, or *hybrid vigor*. In this case the hybrid offspring show a remarkable change from their parents; they will show a greater vitality, more sturdiness, better resistance, and are frequently larger in size. However, hybrid vigor declines in subsequent generations.

Ch. Alsteed's Gretel and Alsteed's Hansel; owner Miss Alma Steedman of New Jersey.

Batzenhof's Piefke, ML; owner Adalbert von Gontard of St. Louis, Mo.
Photo by Kurt E. Mickley.

A specialized type of inbreeding is *linebreeding*. Here all offspring are related to the most desirable, prepotent ancestor. In this way a breeder may produce better results for a certain favorable and admirable characteristic.

Another frequent term is *back-crossing*, which is sometimes called *top-crossing* by animal breeders and *grading* by geneticists.

For the sake of illustration, let us mate a bitch to a very desirable sire. From the F_1 generation we then select a bitch and mate her to the same sire (or to one from the same purebred strain). With dogs this procedure can also be reversed, namely when a son is *back-crossed* with his dam or aunts.

Now let me give an example and describe it in genetic terms. For this purpose we will go back to the two ancient Egyptian "Dachshunds" with the standing ears. [5] [7]

Of course the answer as to whether there is a surgical or genetic basis for those erect ears will probably not be found. All we can do is speculate. [9] [10] Dr. J. P. Scott, at the Roscoe B. Jackson Laboratory in Bar Harbor, Maine, stated (pers. comm.) that when Cocker Spaniels, with long hanging ears, were crossed with Basenjis, with naturally erect ears. "All the F_1's showed the dropped ear, but not quite so extreme as in the Spaniels. The back-cross to the Basenji showed about 50% erect ears, but in the F_2 generation of more than 70 animals we never got a single animal with the erect ears. We

133

conclude that the erect ear is recessive and probably produced by a combination of at least three genes."

Since it is not readily observable, a dominant trait may hide a recessive trait. Selection against a recessive trait is very difficult, particularly if a very large number of ancestors is used. Especially since there are more heterozygotes it is easier to breed out a dominant trait. Recessive traits can be carried from generation to generation without being discovered. The following table [11] will show statistically how many generations may mask a recessive trait, when all recessive homozygotes (aa) are prevented from reproducing. In this manner hidden recessive genes can be passed on to the next generation.

GENERATIONS :	RECESSIVE HOMOZYGOTES (aa)	HETEROZYGOTES (Aa)	DOMINANT HOMOZYGOTES (AA)
1	25.00	50.00	25.00
2	11.11	44.44	44.44
3	6.25	37.50	56.25
4	4.00	32.00	64.00
5	2.78	27.78	69.44
9	1.00	18.00	81.00
10	.83	16.53	82.64
20	.23	9.07	90.70
30	.10	6.24	93.65
40	.06	4.76	95.18
50	.04	3.84	96.12
100	.01	1.96	98.03

Starting with Mendel's 3 to 1 ratio (actually the F_2 generation of the previous table), we see that in the 100th generation there are still almost 2% heterozygotes that carry the recessive trait. In other words, for the Dachshund breeder it would mean, that if smooth Dachshunds would be bred only to smooth, which is dominant to longhair, there would still be 2% in the 100th generation who would hide the longhair. The table shows that the frequency of the homozygous aa is quickly reduced in the early generations, about half in the 2nd generation and about one quarter in the 3rd generation, etc. However in the later generations selection against a recessive trait is very slow, because its occurrence is more infrequent. This little example also demonstrates why it is so very difficult, if not impossible, to state which Dachshund is a "pure" smooth type and which is not.

*
Principles of Genetics, by Sinnott, Dunn & Dobzhansky, Copyright 1950 *by McGraw Hill Book Company. Used by permission of McGraw Hill Book Company.*

Fritz von Blomberg trains with his co-owner B. J. Smith, while co-owner Patricia Smith of Rhode Island takes picture.

Another condition which might be explained in terms of a recessive inheritance is that of cryptorchidism—the failure of both testes to descend into the scrotum; to some extent the same may hold true for monorchidism —where only one testis fails to descend. The higher temperature of the abdominal cavity as compared to that of the scrotum causes faulty development of the spermatozoa. Therefore cryptorchid dogs are generally sterile, or infertile. The monorchid dog, however is able to reproduce.

Very little scientific work has been done on these subjects with dogs. Dr. Josef Härtl's[12] report on research on German Boxers suggests that such an occurrence can be explained by Mendel's 3 to 1 ratio; Dr. Härtl writes that there must be many dominant homozygous female animals that are responsible for many sound offspring. But one can suspect that certain females may be homozygous recessive when there are many cryptorchids among their offspring. He cites, however, the work on goats by Lush, Jonas, and Dammeron, who suggest that there are at least two pairs of "factors" responsible for cryptorchidism.

Dr. Härtl also reports on other research where this condition was investigated and on mammals other than dogs. Elephants are among the few exceptions where cryptorchidism is not a defect, since in elephants the testes never descend into the scrotum. In rabbits the testes descend only during

135

Smooth and longhaired littermates at four months of age. Cora v. Hohenhorst is the longhaired sister of smooth Caro v. Hohenhorst. Co-owners Dr. and Mrs. Helmut E. Adler. Photo by Queens-Nassau Pix.

mating time; in apes and rats the descent is not yet complete at birth.

Dr. Terry Pullig[13], working with Cocker Spaniels, formulated the questions to be answered by future research as follows: "These data indicate that cryptorchidism is inherited as a recessive sex-linked character to the normal descent of the testes in Cocker Spaniels. There are several questions which require more data in order to arrive at anything resembling a satisfactory explanation of cryptorchidism, such as: (1) Are monorchidism and cryptorchidism produced by the same gene, but with varying expressivity? (2) Are they produced by the same gene, but with modifying factors producing the variation? Or (3) are there two different alleles for the two conditions with cryptorchidism dominant to monorchidism?"

Marca Burns[14] advances one remedy for cryptorchidism: "operative removal of the concealed testes." In some cases hormone treatment has proven successful. However, from a breeder's point of view any kind of

Smooth and Wire littermates: Vom Fürstenfels' Kümmel, Knirps and Krümel; breeder-owner Anneliese Wurm of Germany. Photo by same.

treatment is no solution and is to be rejected. No treatment will have any influence on the genetic factors of these conditions. It is therefore important to the breeder not to breed with any bloodlines of known cryptorchids or monorchids.

Often it happens that a trait is dependent on more than one pair of genes. In such a case, one pair, or several pairs, of genes are masked. The dominant pair is said to be *epistatic* over the other pairs. Dr. Clarence C. Little[15] explains this term as "placed above." The masked pair, or pairs, are identified as *hypostatic;* Dr. Little interprets this term as "standing under." To make it even more clear he gives the following example: "In a series of three, there will be a top ranking member, epistatic to both the others; a middle member, hypostatic to the top member but epistatic to the other member; and the bottom member, which is hypostatic to both partners."

It is obvious that this brings up a subject which is very important to the breeder of Dachshunds: the dominance of coat variety.

Prof. Öjvind Winge[16] explained it in the following way:

Wirehair is due to the gene "W." It conceals, or masks, both smooth ("S") and longhair. Smooth in turn can mask longhair. To explain the

Ch. Corlew's Abagail; judge H. Hoch. Co-owners Ruth A. Corpron and Ruth A. Lewis, both of Louisiana; handler Lorraine Heichel. Photo by Ritter.

Ch. Pondwicks Christmas Star; judge Tom Rainey. Co-owners Major and Mrs. Albert I. Stancliff of Arkansas. Handler Roy Murray. Photo by Morry Twomey.

three coat varieties we have to work with two pairs of genes. In this case the following possibilities exist:

Wire = WWSS, WWSs, WWss, WwSS, Ww Ss, or Wwss

Smooth = wwSS or wwSs

Long = wwss

Much more complicated, though, is the analysis of coat color in Dachshunds. The most common colors are red, black-and-tan, and brown, but dappled and wild-colored Dachshunds are also seen.

Since the formulas for the different coat colors are very complicated[17] and too technical to go into deeply here, it is best to give instead a simple list stating essential breeding rules[18]:

Brown x brown	gives only brown
Black x black	gives either only black or 75% black and 25% brown

Ch. Von Relgib's Apollo; judge George Spradling. Owner-handler Ethel Bigler of California. Photo by Bennett Associates.

Red x red	can give all colors, but gives at least 75% red
Wild-colored x wild-colored (sometimes called "salt-and-pepper")	gives either only wild-colored or 75% wild-colored and 25% black or brown
Wild-colored x black or brown	gives either only wild-colored or 50% wild-colored and 50% black or brown
Wild-colored x red	gives either only red or 50% red, at least 25% wild-colored, and the rest black or brown

So far we discussed only genetic assortment in heredity. Nevertheless occasional mutations do occur. It may happen that because of a chemical reaction or radiation, the structure of a gene may change. This change is called *mutation*. The mutated genes, though now exerting a different hereditary influence, still reproduce in the same way as normal genes.

BEHAVIOR GENETICS

It is not only structure and color that are transmitted by the genes but also certain "tendencies" are inherited. For instance, there may be a hereditary predisposition to some diseases. Intelligence also seems to have a hereditary factor. And most recently, geneticists have found that there are definite behavior patterns which are carried from generation to generation. In all of these aspects the environmental conditions are of great importance, exerting a definite influence on the genetically based behavior pattern.

One of the foremost geneticists, Theodosius Dobzhansky[19], expresses his thought as follows: "I certainly do not maintain that the nature—nurture problem is meaningless and that all human variation is always due as much

Ch. K-Hart's Favorite Honey Bun (top winning Dachshund in Canada in 1967; under judge Edward McQuow. Owner Francis Hart of Oklahoma; handler Virginia McCoy. Photo by Morry Twomey.

HOUND GROUP

to heredity as to environment. But to make the distinction between genetic and environmental effects on the phenotype meaningful, the problem must be stated with greater care than it often is.

"It is easy to observe that some people have dark and others light skins; some enjoy robust health and others are handicapped in various ways; some are bright and others dull; some have kindly and others irascible dispositions. Skin pigmentation, health, intelligence and temperament are all, like life itself, necessarily determined by the interaction of the genotypes with their environments."

Even though Dr. Dobzhansky speaks of humans, the same concepts apply to dogs.

The stress not only on environment in its relation to heredity but also on learning and its behavioral aspects are advocated by Dr. Theodore C. Schneirla[20], one of the most outstanding present-day comparative psychologists (a psychologist investigating the behavior pattern of many different

Ch. Hardway Victoria; judge Carol Duffy. Owner-handler Dee Hutchinson of New York. Photo by William P. Gilbert.

Ch. Eronis Heideroeslein L.; judge Ernest Masson. Owner-handler Mrs. Jan Sinore of Georgia. Photo by Earl Graham.

animal species). Dr. Schneirla points out that behavior patterns are not inherited as such, but result from an intimate fusion of genetic factors and environmental effects in development. So close and so complex is this interrelationship at all stages, he points out, that the roles of both genetic factors and of experience must be admitted as essential for all behavior. The role of the standard species environment—although often taken for granted—is no less vital than that of species genetics, if behavior is to turn out normally. The factors of experience range from effects of maternal health and well-being, influential in early physiology, to occurrences leading to simple and complex learning.

In the field of genetics of behavior much research with dogs, among others, was conducted by Drs. John Paul Scott[21] and John L. Fuller at their unique research station at Bar Harbor, Me.

Attempting to learn how much of the dog's behavior is native and how much is the result of his human environment was one important phase of

Charzan's Sabrina Fair, blue longhaired Standard Dachshund; judge Haskill Shuffman. Owner-handler Pat Kennedy of Pennsylvania. Photo by William P. Gilbert.

these studies. To investigate this aspect of behavior, groups of adult dogs were placed in large fields where they could be watched. It was observed that they reacted toward each other with the same basic behavior patterns which they displayed toward people: they wagged their tails, they growled and barked, and they fawned on any animal with food. All these behavior patterns were recorded for later analysis. It was found that the dogs' behavior was essentially the same as that exhibited by their wild ancestors, the wolves. Offspring of these groups of observed dogs showed the same behavior as the adults. But when raised without human contact, the puppies were extremely wild and fearful of people. Literally, the puppies had gone back to a wild state in just one generation.

From this experiment on the nature of learned fears, it was hypothesized that once a puppy had developed timidity, the friendly attitude of their parents had little effect in overcoming it. In other words, each puppy had to learn to fear or not to fear, regardless of the attitude of his elders.

The experiment described above is only one of dozens of traits tested and measured. For instance, early behavior of puppies was tested. Contrary to expectations, the early behavior of puppies was extremely variable. Only after several weeks of repetition and training did their behavior become consistent.

From such studies it was concluded that though heredity may limit the behavioral capacities of animals (dogs, for example, cannot fly), it does not limit their behavior pattern. It is the habit formation which tends to make behavior consistent and invariable. Heredity can act only as a modifier of variability or habit formation.

To investigate deeper into hereditary capacities, tests were set up to measure abilities (like jumping or climbing), thresholds (limits of capacity), or motivation (the wish to perform), and adaptability (to different environments).

Dr. J. P. Scott summarized that "the cross-breeding experiments show that under carefully controlled environmental conditions some behavior traits segregate in accordance with the laws of Mendelian heredity, although even under these conditions there is considerable environmental variability. Most traits are affected by more than one hereditary factor or gene . . ."

Exactly how these traits are inherited, or on which chromosome they are carried, is still open for future geneticists to investigate. Then kennel owners can profit by these experiments and findings and apply them in practice.

REFERENCES CITED
1. Matthew, W. D. 1930. The phylogeny of dogs, *J. Mammal.*, II:117-138.
2. Lorenz, K. 1952. *King Solomon's Ring.* Crowell.
3. Mathey, R. 1954. Chromosomes et systematique des canides, *Mammalia*, 18:225-230.
4. Winge, O. 1950. *Inheritance in Dogs.* Comstock Publishing Co. p. 4.
5. Griffith, F. L. (Ed.) 1893. *Beni Hasan. Archeological Survey of Egypt*, Vol. 1. Kegan, Paul, Trench, Trübner, and Co., London.
6. Hilzheimer, M. 1931. Aus der Stammesgeschichte des Haushundes unter besonderer Berücksichtigung verschiedener Hundetypen. *Z. f. Hundeforschung*, Vol. 1, pp. 3-14.
7. Griffith, F. L. (Ed.), op. cit. 1900, Vol. 4.
8. Burns, M. 1952. *The Genetics of the Dog.* Commonwealth Agriculture Bureaux, England, p. 34.
9. Adler, L. L. 1961. Kommt der Ahnherr des Teckels aus Aegypten? *Der Dachshund*, 16 (5): 107-110.
10. —— 1961. Old Egypt knew various dog breeds, *Pure-bred Dogs*, 78 (Nov.): 18-20, 31.
11. Sinnott, E. W., L. C. Dunn, and T. Dobzhansky. 1950. *Principles of Genetics.* McGraw-Hill Book Co. pp. 319-320.

Ch. Fortune Cookie of Leonca; judge Mrs. O. J. S. de Brun. Co-owners Mrs. Leon Johnson (breeder) and Howard Atlee (handler). Photo by William P. Gilbert.

12. Härtl, J. 1938. Die Vererbung des Kryptorchismus beim Hund, *Zeit. Kleintierkunde und Pelztierkunde "Kleintier und Peltztier,"* 14 (1): 1-37.
13. Pullig, T. 1953. Cryptorchidism in Cocker Spaniels, *J. Heredity*, 44: 250, 264.
14. Burns, M. op. cit. pp. 15-16.
15. Little, C. C. 1957. *Inheritance of Coat Color in Dogs.* Cornell University Press. p. 16.
16. Winge, O. op. cit. p. 136.
17. Little, C. C. op. cit. pp. 131-134.
18. Winge, O. op. cit. p. 144.
19. Dobzhansky, T. 1962. *Mankind Evolving.* Yale University Press. p. 44.
20. Schneirla, T. C. 1955. "Interrelationships of the 'innate' and the 'acquired' in the instinctive behavior", in *L'instinct dans le Comportment des Animeaux et de l'Homme.* Masson. pp. 387-452.
21. Scott, J. P. 1958. *Animal Behavior.* University of Chicago Press. pp. 114, 122-124.

Chapter IV

Breeding Particulars

PRELIMINARY DISCUSSION

We have seen many Dachshund kennels come and go. Many started with a big bang only to fizzle out after a few years. Again, others began small, stayed small, and disappeared unnoticed from the scene. Only a tiny percentage of breeders scored success after success. Mostly it was those who started modestly and went their own way in a determined manner without being unduly influenced, but with an inborn sense for acute observations of nature. It was these breeders who won real success, not just ribbons, and who remained ever faithful to the breed.

To be done with it, let us say here: the only true and untarnishable reward for the endless labor that is connected with a substantial kennel is the artistic satisfaction derived from the creation of some—always only a few—really highly perfected animals. Everything else, in the end, is gross self-deception. Success in field trials or even at dog shows cannot, in the long run, satisfy a reasoning person. These successes can only have value in confirming to the breeder, by comparison, whether his breeding efforts are correct, and whether he does not over- or under-estimate his labors as a breeder. Therefore these successes can never be an end in themselves, they can only have value on a comparative scale. Show prizes and trophies, which are most often only a pitiful return in value, considering the expenses, for the time involved and the danger of dogs catching contagious diseases, are not as satisfying as the knowledge that "you are on the right track with your stock."

SHOULD I BECOME A DACHSHUND BREEDER?

Innumerable times the question has been asked: "What do you think, I would also once like to try my hand in breeding Dachshunds; would you advise me to do it?" The answer was most often guarded and laconic: "I don't know." If the questioners could not be put off with this answer, they were given the philosophy outlined in the first two paragraphs of this chapter.

Ch. De Sangpur Mr. Special; judge George Plumber. Co-owners Ann and Sid (handler) Sims of Texas. Photo by Morry Twomey.

If anybody believed that he could find satisfaction in dog clubs or at regular meetings, the most honest reply was: "In any other club you would find, in the long run, more relaxation and pleasures. A dog club is—to use some 'big' words—usually a conglomeration of the most heterogeneous elements. Very few of the members have any interest in the scientific basis of breeding. Lack of understanding, mania for apparent successes, envy, jealousy, squabbles and dissension, thrive almost no place as well as in a dog club. The old German phrase: 'Breeding dogs spoils the character', is not always unjustified. The most serious and successful breeder—who does not bother with distracting amusements and club activities, which only too often take on much importance—has little company or often stands alone; in the long run anyway."

Some people are blinded by some fantastic prices paid here or there for a Dachshund. They ask naïvely: "What do you think, could one have quite a good second income from breeding Dachshunds?" Again an honest reply would be: "Certainly not on a continuous basis or in an absolutely decent way." If commercial breeding is carried on obstinately, anyway, for decades by many people, and these people talk themselves into believing that they "made a profit," then this is a terrible self-deception. These people figure falsely; they are blind to the continuous expenses, which they either do not realize or else do not want to admit to themselves. Above everything, they do not figure the valuable time which is lost to their profession and maybe also to their families. But it is like horse-trading, people just cannot stop it even·if they could make a better and more honest living elsewhere! Shockingly high is the number of acquaintances who deteriorated economically and morally or even were totally ruined because of the dog fancy. The kennel name *Mon malheur* ("My Bad Luck") turned out to be the sad truth for many. If you do not want to breed your dogs quietly for yourself, if you want to venture out onto the thin ice of dog politics, then, dear friend, be prepared for the worst! If you are enough of a cynic and if you have a sound and good common sense, then you may dare it anyway. But from the start, do not expect either satisfaction or "pure joy." These attributes you find more surely elsewhere, at least in the long run. If you want pure pleasure from your dogs, then breed only for yourself, and as little as possible!

For breeding, dear beginner, you need above all three things: time—much time—money, and an inborn talent. And of each, much more than you would believe. If your job and your economic station allows you ample leisure, so that you do not have to neglect your daily duties, then you may venture it; especially if you can be moderate in your hobbies, and if your

Ch. Rose Farm's Moon Rockette; judge Muriel Newhauser. Owner-handler Dee Hutchinson of New York. Photo by Stephen Klein.

family shows understanding, assuming, of course, that you have some talent for breeding! The city dweller should think it over three times. If he does not have good food sources, accommodating neighbors, and enough space for runs, he might as well keep his hands off breeding and be satisfied with *one* Dachshund. There have been cases where the family bathtub had to serve as a nursery for puppies. To raise dogs in apartments makes a lot of dirt and is like punishment for Dachshunds. It may also be the cause of gradual deficiency diseases. Equally as objectionable is mass-breeding in the city, possibly yet in tight quarters.

If the city dweller wants to have a substantial kennel, even though he has neither ample open space and sufficient time for plenty of activity and work with his dogs, then he must "farm" several of them out into the suburbs or nearby villages. He will have to find out where he can let the weaned puppies grow up, either alone, or two of them together, at most in threes, in a place where they will get much fresh air, sun, and, if possible, much freedom. Such an assignment has the advantage that the custodian, if he is also an animal lover, can devote more time to the individual dog. Also in this way the intellectual powers are stimulated more. Above all the dread dis-

Ch. Villanol's Wee Mignon; judge Mrs. Iola W. Pflueger. Owner-handler Gordon Carvill of New York. Photo by William P. Gilbert.

Robdachs Love of Mallet Creek (nearly finished); judge Grace Hirshman. Co-owners Sanford L. and Patricia Roberts (handling) of California. Photo by Alfred Stillman.

temper will not spread as easily, a disease that is a scourge, particularly of our purebred dogs, so prone to its ravages. Actually, only the huntsman should devote himself to Dachshund breeding. He alone is in a position to bring out in the Dachshund all of its latent talent, both mental and physical. He alone is capable of pursuing truly high grade breeding. The huntsman, if he is a sociable person, will always find a farmer in the villages within his district, who would not mind raising one or two Dachshunds. Inside the preserve there is always something to do for the young Dachshund. Here, one can let him stir up a rabbit; there, one can shoot a squirrel in front of him, which the dog can finish off; and in addition one can make a little drag-hunt with it, etc. This is real Dachshund raising! This method produces the heartiest, the toughest, and the most efficient Dachshunds.

HOW SHOULD I START BREEDING?

When you believe that you can satisfy preliminary conditions: healthful food and sufficiently sunny quarters and runs, then you can acquire one, and *only one* bitch, two to three years old. If you are a beginner, be sure to take the advice of an experienced breeder. It is absolutely unnecessary that yours be a highly-bred or prize-winning bitch. Health and merit of the dam are more valuable than outstanding beauty. We have often seen that the queen of the ball is by no means always also a good mother. The bitch should not be young, in order that her childhood diseases be behind her! Should she have already raised a litter, so much the better. The second litter is usually easier to raise. Many beginners like to buy a bitch because she is registered; they think that thus they receive the stamp of approval of the breed and nothing could go wrong. Nothing could be more fatal than such a belief. A studbook is nothing less than a book of "Who's Who." Studbooks also register Dachshunds with bad faults, even those with a whole bunch of shortcomings.

Every breeder knows that at eight to ten months of age bad faults can still show up. Knuckling especially is seldom apparent before the sixth month, and often much later. One should not breed with such dogs; at least, the beginner should not do that. The usual studbook has in no way the

Ch. Muselands' Alysia shown receiving BOV, and BOS to BOB at 1st Knickerbocker Dachshund Club Specialty, under judge Mrs. Robert Lindsey. Looking on is Howard Atlee president of K.D.C., while Patricia Beresford Fowler presents the trophy. Owner Dorothy A. Muse of Tennessee; handler Bobby B. Barlow. Photo by William P. Gilbert.

Ch. Robdachs Familiar Stranger, BOB at 1st Knickerbocker D.C. Specialty, is shown winning BOV under judge Dr. Sterling Brown. Presenting trophy is Mary Castoral. Co-owners Sanford L. and Patricia A. Roberts of California; handler James Swyler. Photo by William P. Gilbert.

purpose of registering only valuable dogs—an error, which is, regrettably, still wide-spread. Likewise, a prize won at a dog show is by no means a guarantee of the quality of the dog for breeding purposes. To repeat again: the beginner should let a reliable expert, who is himself an experienced breeder, counsel him in a purchase. A stud dog should not be bought by a beginner, because the best sires are not for sale; and if they are, then only for a very stiff price. For breeding, the best sire is just good enough. In such a choice, the beginner should again seek careful advice.

If the bitch has a long pedigree, so much the better. But it is only of value if it contains well-known, excellent dogs. The mere mentioning of names will not do a thing. From the pedigree, the characteristics of the ancestors have to be recognized, at least of the parents, grandparents, and great-grandparents: distinctions won at exhibitions, dog shows, and field trials. The last one is the most important if the offspring are to be used for hunting. Furthermore there should be a description of weight, chest circumference, variety, and color.

The same goes for the pedigree of the stud dog. He should by all means have passed tests for work in dens and in trailing, and if possible also such other areas as tracking, ability to work in water, and different tasks in obedience. The more versatile and capable the sire is, the better. Even those who do not hunt should appreciate its importance if only in the interest of the breed. It is these achievement awards which point to health, energy, and intelligence. A dog and a breed cannot have enough of these attributes. Dachshunds who are indifferent to hunting, or even cold, are more likely to transmit apathy, timidity, and denseness, all characteristics which lead to a mental degeneration of the breed. Whoever breeds hunting dogs also has the moral duty to work for the conservation of the hunting characteristics of the breed. The most beautiful stud dog of a working breed harms the breed if he is worthless for work; especially when his "achievements" only consist of eating, stud service, strolling, or lying around. Whoever recommends or uses stud dogs, but does not want to, or cannot, enter field trials, only harms the breed. If dogs are put in this world who will amount to little or nothing, then complaints are bound to start, not only concerning these

Ch. Delldachs Wanda the Witch W.; judge Alice Marie Cornet. Owner-handler Eunice Huffman of South Carolina. Photo by Stephen Klein.

Ch. Eronis Esprit De Corps L.; judge Mrs. Gus Meyer. Co-owners Mr. and Mrs. Terry W. Sinore of Georgia; handler Mr. Sinore. Photo by Morry Twomey.

wrongly bred dogs, but about the entire breed. The Augean Stables of the Dachshund breed miss the refreshing roughness of a Hegewald who is reported to have said once, with reference to a dog with a poor nose: "Take this dog shooting, replace the 'oo' with 'it,' and you'll find out where his talent lies."

You should not pay attention to the usual talk: "My dog is very keen, all he needs is exercise and opportunity." Such assertions are no proof; least of all in the working Dachshund circles!

The more high awards in conformation and achievement the ancestors can show, so much the better; especially on the dam's side, whose primary role in breeding for achievement is still not taken sufficiently into consideration. The better established good characteristics are in the bloodlines, the more surely they will be passed on.

A big, maybe the biggest, disadvantage of studbooks is that they do not record anything on the faults of the dogs. Yet, it is of special importance to know these faults. Therefore you have to inquire personally, or with the help of an expert, about possible faults of the stud himself and of his ancestors. The individual animal is not at all the true image of its genetic potential. On the contrary, it can carry characteristics which never become apparent (latent, hidden characteristics), but which were present in the parents, the grandparents, etc., and which can show up again in his progeny.

KENNEL LOG BOOK

One should have a personal kennel log book. One should make extensive notes on the pedigree and the faults and merits, both physically and mentally, of home-bred dogs. Then, eventually, the kennel log book can fill the gap in the studbooks. A long-range breeding program can be based with much more confidence on one's own, rather extensively kept, kennel pedigree, than on the general studbooks. Due to their nature, these studbooks can only register the most meager information. After five to ten years of breeding the extensive personal studbook will have acquired an outstanding value for breeding purposes. Never, though, should one be blind to the faults of one's own dogs.

Ch. Wilheen's Wee Annette, MW; judge Lt.-Col. W. Pede. Co-owners Ruth A. Corpron and Ruth A. Lewis (handler) of Louisiana. Photo by Morry Twomey.

Ch. Von Relgib's Beauty of Bardale; judge Harold Bishop. Owner Barbara J. Gralheer of Kansas; handler R. Richard Leap. Photo by Morry Twomey.

WHEN SHOULD THE BITCH BE BRED?

Provided that you have a capable brood bitch, and provided you have made the earliest possible arrangements for the most fitting stud dog, then you have to decide at which heat of the bitch would it be best to breed her. In general, the bitch comes into season twice a year. Although there are absolutely healthy bitches who come into heat only once a year, this is rare. This occurrence is probably a throwback to the ancestral origin of the dogs, the wild canines. The wolf, for instance, whelps only once a year. This is assumedly because raising cubs in the winter would be too difficult due to the weather and the scarcity of food. Therefore whelping occurs in the spring. Accordingly, most bitches come into heat between December and February; in this way the puppies arrive in early spring and can develop well in the open air during the summer. After about six months, the bitches will come into season again, making it about the middle of summer, June to August; so that she would whelp in the fall. It is obvious that it is preferable to use the heat which brings the litter in the spring. If, however, a warm and roomy kennel is available, then the second heat can be used. Puppies are apparently not more prone to diseases in winter. Some of the most terrible distemper attacks, which destroyed an entire stock of puppies, have occurred in the hottest summer months. Of course, you have to give puppies ample opportunity to exercise in winter, whenever the weather is dry and sunny. You have to see that the stall, as well as the kennel, is absolutely dry; that the best straw for bedding is used; and that good, warm food is offered several times a day. One advantage of winter puppies is that they are not as much bothered by insect pests, and the flies spread no diseases.

It goes without saying that the bitch is bred only once a year. However, you should not skip more than two heats, generally speaking, between breedings, since then the bitch may have trouble becoming impregnated.

The first season usually occurs between seven to nine months of age. Since the bitch is not yet fully developed, it is advisable not to breed at this time.

Ch. Holow's Dancing Doll L.; judge C. Burian. Owner-handler Evelyn F. Boyer of Maryland. Photo by Evelyn M. Shafer.

Ch. Holow's Crown Jewel L.; judge Alice Marie Cornet. Co-owners Evelyn and Wilfred (handler) Boyer of Maryland. Photo by Evelyn M. Shafer.

RECOGNITION OF THE HEAT

The first sign of the oncoming heat is the restless and lively behavior of the bitch. She jumps on other dogs and her outer genitalia swell up. Later, drops of blood are discharged from the vagina and one says the bitch "stains." The most perfect time for mating is generally the seventh or eighth day after onset of staining. If you want to ship the bitch to the stud dog, then you should make sure previously that she will "stand," that is, accept the male. As a test, bring in a dog on a leash; if the bitch stands and holds her tail to the side, then it is the correct time to ship her. Many owners ship their bitches as soon as the first traces of the heat appear; then they leave it up to the owner of the stud dog to determine when the bitch is ready to stand. Naturally, the greatest care should be taken during the heat, as well as before and after mating, that no other dog comes near the bitch. Otherwise the owner would be cheated of realizing his hopes with regard to the expected litter. The best thing is to keep the bitch securely guarded during the entire time. If you do not have any trustworthy assistants, then it is better to take care of her feeding yourself, since possibly other dogs which are present may not waste any opportunity to force their way into the stall and to pay a visit to the bitch. The guarding and care of a strange bitch is a great burden for the owner of the stud dog; especially since many bitches howl day and night because they are lonely for their owners. Therefore you should not ship her off too soon, but, on the other hand, not one day too late. For it is annoying for the owner of the stud dog to find out that the bitch will no longer stand. Inexperienced and malicious owners of bitches are then quickly ready with their absurd reproach: "The stud dog is no good!"

Bitches that tend to snap must be announced beforehand so that essential precautions can be taken for their arrival—if necessary with a muzzle.

Whoever owns a kennel will undoubtedly have available enough space, which can be sufficiently closed off, for bitches in season. The shipment has to be made in a more or less closed crate or carrying case rather than in a

Ch. Pruitt's Charly; judge Lyman R. Fisher. Co-owners Margaret and Henry Pruitt of Florida; handler Bennie L. Dennard Sr. Photo by Earl Graham.

Ch. Wag's Sprinwire; judge Mrs. Albert E. (Ramona) Van Court. Co-owners Bill and Tommie (handling) Stewart of California. Photo by Henry C. Schley.

cage with widely spaced bars. It is certainly sufficient if the act of mating is accomplished only once. One mating would be enough to fertilize many thousands of ova, if the bitch would have that many available. There are some ignorant people who, in spite of everything, retain the opinion that the number of puppies depends also on the stud dog. This is absolute non-sense, because the number of puppies depends simply and solely on the mother. One stud dog was accused of being no good because the bitch had only two puppies in her litter. By chance, eight days later another bitch serviced by the same stud dog threw eleven puppies. This is an exceptionally high number for a Dachshund bitch. This same bitch delivered nine puppies fathered by another sire. In general one can say: the bigger the bitch, probably the larger the litter. It is well known that Pointers and Setters throw bigger litters than Dachshunds. And among the Dachshunds the Miniatures have fewer puppies than the larger type. Some Dachshund bitches have, almost regularly, three, others four, and still others six puppies. The first litter of a bitch is usually small. More than six puppies in a Dachshund litter is a rather infrequent occurrence.

Just to make absolutely sure, your stud dog should cover the bitches twice for the first time they are mated. Furthermore, it should be pointed out that the bitch, on arrival, should be allowed to rest for several hours before mating to let her become accustomed to her new surroundings.

It happens sometimes that a bitch will not accept a dog. In that case you have to separate the two. The next day or, if necessary, the day after, you can let another available leashed dog go to her carefully, until she stands. Only then, should you reintroduce the stud dog designated for her. Bitches that do not stand readily will generally bite the stud dog viciously, if there are too many unsuccessful tries. However, when a new stud dog makes his appearance, she may stand readily and willingly. The same thing is true for stud dogs. After unsuccessfully trying for several days with an uncooperative bitch, he may lose interest at times, but will still court a newly arriving bitch immediately and eagerly. The number of lazy and clumsy stud dogs is high, especially in Dachshunds. In most dogs, though, their eagerness increases with age.

How long the dogs are locked is rather unimportant for the success of the act. It also happens, and not infrequently, that they do not lock at all but the bitch still becomes pregnant.

Before the age of one and a half years, a dog should not be used for stud; if for no other reason that you cannot form a final opinion of his merits.

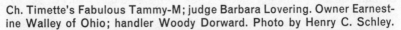

Ch. Timette's Fabulous Tammy-M; judge Barbara Lovering. Owner Earnestine Walley of Ohio; handler Woody Dorward. Photo by Henry C. Schley.

Mating and Whelping Calendar

(63 Day Gestation Period)

January Bred	March Whelped	February Bred	April Whelped	March Bred	May Whelped	April Bred	June Whelped	May Bred	July Whelped	June Bred	August Whelped	July Bred	September Whelped	August Bred	October Whelped	September Bred	November Whelped	October Bred	December Whelped	November Bred	January Whelped	December Bred	February Whelped
1	5	1	5	1	3	1	3	1	3	1	3	1	2	1	3	1	3	1	3	1	3	1	2
2	6	2	6	2	4	2	4	2	4	2	4	2	3	2	4	2	4	2	4	2	4	2	3
3	7	3	7	3	5	3	5	3	5	3	5	3	4	3	5	3	5	3	5	3	5	3	4
4	8	4	8	4	6	4	6	4	6	4	6	4	5	4	6	4	6	4	6	4	6	4	5
5	9	5	9	5	7	5	7	5	7	5	7	5	6	5	7	5	7	5	7	5	7	5	6
6	10	6	10	6	8	6	8	6	8	6	8	6	7	6	8	6	8	6	8	6	8	6	7
7	11	7	11	7	9	7	9	7	9	7	9	7	8	7	9	7	9	7	9	7	9	7	8
8	12	8	12	8	10	8	10	8	10	8	10	8	9	8	10	8	10	8	10	8	10	8	9
9	13	9	13	9	11	9	11	9	11	9	11	9	10	9	11	9	11	9	11	9	11	9	10
10	14	10	14	10	12	10	12	10	12	10	12	10	11	10	12	10	12	10	12	10	12	10	11
11	15	11	15	11	13	11	13	11	13	11	13	11	12	11	13	11	13	11	13	11	13	11	12
12	16	12	16	12	14	12	14	12	14	12	14	12	13	12	14	12	14	12	14	12	14	12	13
13	17	13	17	13	15	13	15	13	15	13	15	13	14	13	15	13	15	13	15	13	15	13	14
14	18	14	18	14	16	14	16	14	16	14	16	14	15	14	16	14	16	14	16	14	16	14	15
15	19	15	19	15	17	15	17	15	17	15	17	15	16	15	17	15	17	15	17	15	17	15	16
16	20	16	20	16	18	16	18	16	18	16	18	16	17	16	18	16	18	16	18	16	18	16	17
17	21	17	21	17	19	17	19	17	19	17	19	17	18	17	19	17	19	17	19	17	19	17	18
18	22	18	22	18	20	18	20	18	20	18	20	18	19	18	20	18	20	18	20	18	20	18	19
19	23	19	23	19	21	19	21	19	21	19	21	19	20	19	21	19	21	19	21	19	21	19	20
20	24	20	24	20	22	20	22	20	22	20	22	20	21	20	22	20	22	20	22	20	22	20	21
21	25	21	25	21	23	21	23	21	23	21	23	21	22	21	23	21	23	21	23	21	23	21	22
22	26	22	26	22	24	22	24	22	24	22	24	22	23	22	24	22	24	22	24	22	24	22	23
23	27	23	27	23	25	23	25	23	25	23	25	23	24	23	25	23	25	23	25	23	25	23	24
24	28	24	28	24	26	24	26	24	26	24	26	24	25	24	26	24	26	24	26	24	26	24	25
25	29	25	29	25	27	25	27	25	27	25	27	25	26	25	27	25	27	25	27	25	27	25	26
26	30	26	30	26	28	26	28	26	28	26	28	26	27	26	28	26	28	26	28	26	28	26	27
27	31	27	May 1	27	29	27	29	27	29	27	29	27	28	27	29	27	29	27	29	27	29	27	28
28	April 1	28	2	28	30	28	30	28	30	28	30	28	29	28	30	28	30	28	30	28	30	28	Mar 1
29	2			29	31	29	July 1	29	31	29	31	29	30	29	31	29	Dec 1	29	31	29	31	29	2
30	3			30	June 1	30	2	30	Aug 1	30	Sept 1	30	Oct 1	30	Nov 1	30	2	30	Jan 1	30	Feb 1	30	3
31	4			31	2			31	2			31	2	31	2			31	2			31	4

Ch. Nixon's Forest Sprite, one of the top brood bitches in the United States is owned and handled by Dr. C. William Nixon of Massachussetts.

With Miniature Dachshunds, who are fully developed much more quickly and who are more precocious, one year is old enough for dogs and bitches. This precociousness makes up for the somewhat reduced number of puppies in this type.

There are people who think that once a bitch is mated to a purebred stud dog, it would not be so bad if she is immediately mated thereafter to an unwanted dog. This is absolutely false. Research in this area (Engelmann, 1896, in the *Zeitschrift für Biologie* ["Journal for Biology"]) has conclusively shown that the following can occur when a bitch mates with two different dogs in succession: 1. The bitch delivers puppies only from the first dog; 2. she delivers puppies only from the second dog; 3. she delivers puppies from both dogs. In such experiments one has to select very different types of sires. In these studies, a white Spitz was selected as the second sire.

Only when the heat is completely finished can you give the bitch free run again.

PREGNANCY

At this time the bitch should be treated as before. She should get good food and sufficient activity. Whether or not a bitch is in whelp, cannot be determined with accuracy during the first four weeks. With some bitches the signs become obvious before; whereas with others there can be doubt about their pregnancy up to the last week. It is even possible that a bitch shows signs of pregnancy but is not even carrying a litter; perhaps because she did not become impregnated or because the fetus died. The bitch may even have milk, but the expected litter does not arrive. Pregnancy lasts from 61 to 65 days, but on the average is usually 63 days. After the first four weeks one should not continue to use the bitch for hunting, especially not for work in dens. The opinion that diligent work during pregnancy would strongly influence the puppies' aptitude for hunting is, to say the least, exaggerated. Whatever was neglected in the ancestry, that is to say, whatever was not securely anchored in the pedigree, cannot at all be made up for in these four short weeks.

WHELPING

At least eight days before the bitch's "due date" prepare a whelping box so that she can become accustomed to using it. There are all kinds of models on the market, most of them expensive. The best and simplest thing is always an ordinary box about 30″ (about 75 cm.) long and about 20″ (about

Start of labor. Photo by R. Insam.

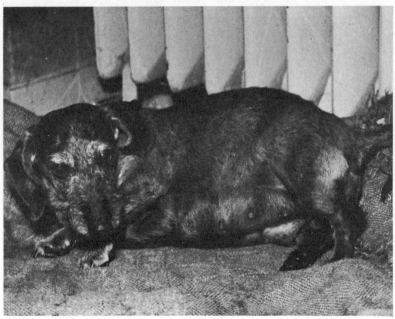

165

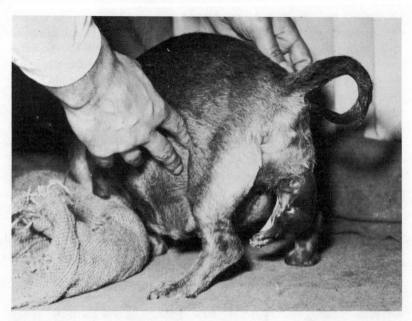

First puppy, breech position, being born in amniotic sac. Photo by R. Insam.

Bitch cleans and dries puppy. Photo by R. Insam.

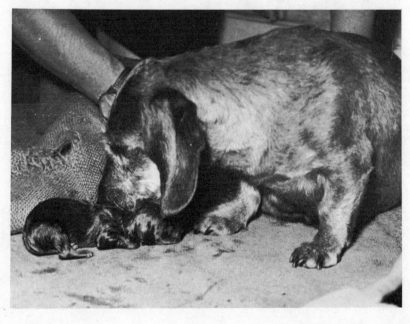

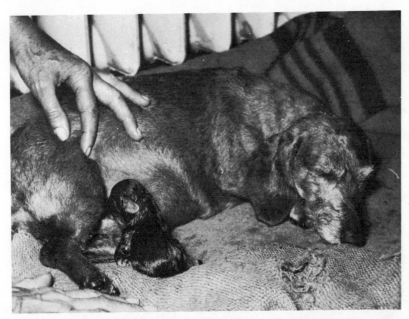

First puppy nurses. Puppies seem to prefer lower nipples. Bitch rests. Photo by R. Insam.

Two puppies have arrived, both are nursing. Photo by R. Insam.

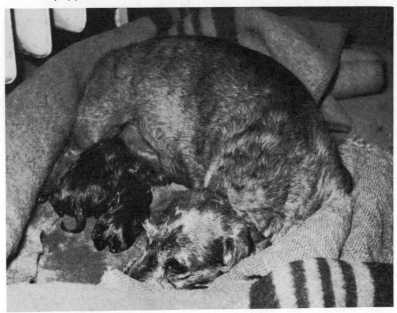

Fifth puppy being born, normal (head first) position, while littermates hold position on nipples. Photo by R. Insam.

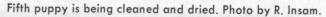

Fifth puppy is being cleaned and dried. Photo by R. Insam.

Close-up of new-born puppy, blunt faced and blind, 30 seconds after birth. Photo by R. Insam.

50 cm.) to 24" (about 60 cm.) wide. It should be no higher than 6" (about 15 cm.), while the front should not exceed 4" (about 10 cm.), so that the brood bitch can comfortably enter the box without having to jump, she might otherwise land too heavily on top of the puppies. If the box is too high there is also the danger that a puppy could get killed. Suppose that a puppy is holding on tightly to a nipple and the dam makes a sudden leap out of the box, he may then be dragged along most violently. Such a situation could occur, should the dam suspect sudden danger from either a strange dog or a strange person.

Naturally, anything that may disturb the dam should be kept away from her.

Straw or similar material in the whelping box is not advised. The bitch always moves everything away so that the puppies will lie on the bare wood.I recommend a double folded piece of burlap on the floor of the box, well secured with large tacks, so that it can be removed easily and cleaned, when necessary.

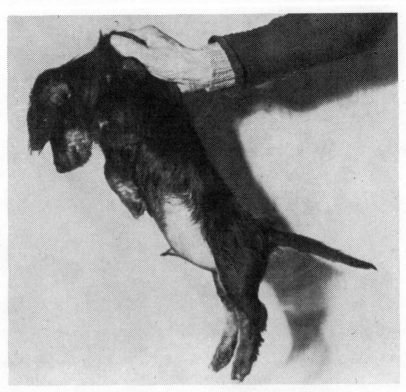

Wrong way to lift a puppy. Photo by R. Insam.

During the delivery the bitch should be left alone. However, if you believe help is needed, a veterinarian should be contacted and asked for advice. Or, if none is available, ask an experienced breeder. Never should a beginner try to help the bitch by manipulation.

Simulated death in puppies. Much too little attention is paid to the question of whether the newly whelped puppy, which is apparently born dead, is really dead. Frequently the so-called dead puppy was removed, although its death was only simulated and with the appropriate manipulation it could have been saved. The careful observer may have noticed the anxious haste with which a good brood bitch throws her seemingly lifeless puppy around. Let her be, even if she is "very rough" with him. She knows what she is doing. If necessary one can help her by giving the puppy artificial respiration by moving him to and fro in the same manner you would grasp a child under the armpits, if you wanted to swing him or her around. Skillfull bitches try to move the tongue forward, of puppies which do not breathe, apparently by licking the inside of their mouths. The mouth also should be freed of mucous. If you can bring yourself to do it, you might try sucking the respiratory organs free. Such a procedure has already brought some valuable puppies back to life. A tongue which is curled back can be brought forward with the curved end of a bobby pin. A breeder once put an apparently dead puppy into the stove right after delivery to burn him. The fire was out though, and before he could get it started again (he was delayed by another birth, from doing it immediately!) the remaining heat in the closed stove had such a beneficial effect on the puppy inside, that it brought him to life and he protested his fiery death with his thin little voice. Therefore do not be too fast to write out the death certificate.

How do you lift a puppy ? The "expert" often makes the observation that people in general are very awkward when they are in the embarrassing situation of having to lift a young dog. You can see how, for example, a person who wants to appear very "matter of fact" will take hold of the little

Right way to lift a puppy. Photo by R. Insam.

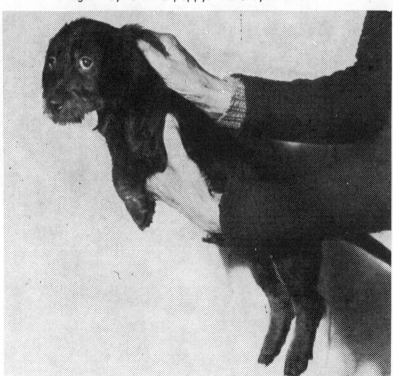

chap with the tips of his thumb and index finger holding him by the scruff of the neck. The innocent victim's eyes threaten to fill with tears because of this treatment and his appearance moves every understanding animal lover. When such unjust treatment is protested, we almost always hear that this is the way it is usually done. This however is not the case. One should grasp with the clenched fist; therefore, on one side with all four fingertips and on the other side the entire length of the thumb (including the muscle of the thumb in the palm). Grasp the nape of the neck of the puppy exactly over the shoulder blades. To give further support while lifting him up place the other hand underneath his chest. In the case of very young puppies, perhaps even new born ones, this method of lifting is not recommended. In such a case push a hand underneath the puppy to raise him. But even for the grown dog, it is better not to lift him with the "neck grasp," and even less to pull him up by his front legs! You can either hold him on both sides with open hands under the elbows or with both hands under the chest. Lifting by the tail, as you see occasionally, is cruel and to be rejected.

Ch. Torals Sweet Bramble nurses her three-week-old litter. Owner Mary Castoral of New York. Photo by Frank Castoral.

Removal of dewclaws. This cockspur of some dogs is simply a necessary accompaniment of these extra appendages at the inside of the hindlegs close to the actual paw. If this toe, which does not have an actual bone structure, is removed within the first few days after birth only one drop of blood is all that will be shed. The dam usually licks it off and thereby will prevent the swelling of the wound and helps the blood to coagulate. In case the dewclaw rests in a lot of skin, first make an incision with sharp scissors between the toe and the leg bone, then clip the dewclaw off, with either sharp pliers or scissors.

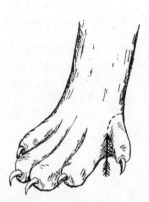

Dewclaw. Arrow shows first incision by removal of dewclaw; dashes show the second incision.

With grown dogs this operation can be done without any difficulty, but should be performed only by a veterinarian. It also occasionally happens that this claw appears in a double edition, both dangling close together.

CHOICE OF PUPPIES

Puppies are born blind and their eyes open only after 10 to 14 days. How many puppies should remain with their dam? Sensibly, the number should be four, because the bitch has four nipples on each side. Therefore she could accommodate four puppies at the same time. Should the choice between four and five puppies be a difficult one to make, then leave it; one more or less will not make that much difference. Naturally, those with faults will be discarded immediately, for example those with flesh-colored noses. It should be remembered though, that chocolate or blue coated Dachshunds always, and dappled Dachshunds frequently have light noses. Besides a light nose often becomes darker in red or black-and-tan Dachshunds. Furthermore, those with too much white should be eliminated. However care should be taken in this matter, because the white on the toes frequently disappears with age, until it has completely vanished. In dappled Dachshunds moderate white markings are not disturbing. In red Dachshunds all kinds of mixtures are possible, from rabbit-gray to a red mixed with much black hair. The final hair colors only arrive with the first hair change. Whereas black-and-tan, dappled, chocolate and blue Dachshunds mostly have their final coat colors at birth. Only very light shades of red (*apricot*, *fawn*, *wheaten*) do not turn later into a deep red color. In the wirehair one recognizes only after weeks, even months, whether the puppies will finally be smooths or wires. As soon as the puppies get their teeth, they should be checked for a possible undershot bite; even though, this fault sometimes straightens itself out later.

FOSTER MOTHERS

If a brood bitch has a very large litter, which is well marked, and because of the parentage presumably represents considerable value, it may become necessary to find a foster mother. In her selection pay especial attention to her health. She should have delivered her own litter only a few days before or after. While the real mother is absent, the puppies should be removed and given to the foster mother; with this procedure there is usually no

Mays' Trampus-M.; owner Mrs. Charlie Mays of California. Photo by Fran Hall.

Togetherness! These two puppies are Remanded Boffin and Remanded Benison. Co-owners Mr. and Mrs. Muller Koeper of Iowa. Photo by George T. Henry.

difficulty in acceptance. Nevertheless, vigilance is advisable. It was noticed repeatedly that brood bitches which had weaned their own young secretly took away a kennel mate's puppies and proceded to nurse them faithfully. It so happened that the longhaired bitch "Ilse I.v. Sonnenstein" raised two puppies perfectly which belonged to the litter of her daughter "Ilse II." Naturally these are chance occurrences with which one cannot figure.

Raising puppies artificially with a milk bottle is a tedious and thankless task; especially since the careful cleaning of puppies by the dam and her warmth are missing. Women generally have more talent and patience for such jobs than men.

THE FIRST FEW MONTHS

The first six weeks present little difficulty to the breeder. The main thing for him is to feed the dam well, if possible with meat and milk. She will take care of everything else. She keeps the puppies immaculately clean and nurses them without trouble if she has from four to five.

Beginning with the fourth week the puppies start to crawl about independently; they also start to take food other than their mother's milk, such as cows milk, rolls, soups, and thin mush. Everything should be served warm; the milk should be thinned from $\frac{1}{3}$ to $\frac{1}{2}$ with water and then boiled. Potatoes or dark bread should not be added yet. Tiny, tender pieces of meat can also be offered; soon they will be eaten more eagerly than anything else; this is a sure sign that the body needs them. Later, of course, meat is and stays the best and most natural food for a dog; it is regrettable that today sufficient amounts can hardly be afforded.

After the sixth week the puppies can be removed from the dam; you should start to sell or give away those you do not want to keep at this point. The rest will be better able to enjoy themselves with their mother, for a few more weeks.

When and which puppies should be sold or given away? This question is always a difficult one to answer. The purpose of breeding is to keep the best of the good ones in order to improve the stock further, if possible. By six or eight weeks even the expert cannot tell which puppy is the best one. If at

One of Mays' Miniatures in a mischievous mood. Owner Mrs. Charlie Mays of California. Photo by Fran Hall.

all possible, keep the puppies till they are $4\frac{1}{2}$ months old. By that time you can judge, to some extent such things as the bite, the ears, and to a certain degree also the coat and color. At times there are puppies with overshot bite who outgrow this condition completely with the change of teeth in the fourth or fifth month. Small white spots on the toes tend to disappear at this age, as already mentioned earlier. The impurities of color in the red Dachshund start to diminish or become permanent, and one can now recognize which puppies will turn out to be good wirehairs. Those puppies, which in the second or third month already have long wire coats most often do not turn out to be the best. Do not be misled at this point to prefer those young dogs which already look more like mature Dachshunds, with a pointed, narrow head, long body etc. It has usually been better to keep those with a somewhat heavier, clumsier head and a plumper, apparently shorter body. This type often develops better later than those whose figures are finished earlier.

Have patience with a faulty tail; as the bones and cartilage harden the tail will also tend to straighten out more.

Least predictable is the stance in the Dachshund. *"Bodenabstand"* ("distance from ground to lowest point of chest") and possible knuckling can most often be determined only after nine months. Especially low and well-rounded chests, with broad front legs set far back are a kind of a stunted puppyhood. In other words; the Dachshund retains the basic shape he had at five to six months; one refers to a "marchpane-piglet" or to a "seal" type then.

However the reverse is true with the aptitude for hunting. There you cannot notice precocity soon enough. Its presence usually points to a definite inherited tendency. Here are some examples of this. A rat in a wiretrap was shown to the smooth "Waldmann" (Dildomde-Fassan bloodlines), when he was three months old. He dragged the trap furiously around. When the rat was released in an empty room, he was caught and finished off pretty quickly. This dog lived up to his early promise; however, he knuckled later, which was very regrettable, and therefore was not used for breeding. The longhaired 4½ months old "Braune Hexe v. Sonnenstein" (*T.St.B.*—Dachshund studbook—2163), a very small bitch, was taken for the first time to a private game preserve, accompanied by two hunters and an older Dachshund, who was not much good. Deer were crossing the fire break in the woods; when the little bitch reached the tracks, she followed them for quite a stretch, giving tongue loudly all the while. Then the party looked over a fox's den, a so-called "eightholer." Before they knew what had happened, the little bitch had disappeared into the den singing out excitedly from inside. Immediately afterwards a fox leaped out of the other end. Before this incident the bitch had had no opportunity to work a den. She too, became an excellent hunting dog, who learned everything by herself and transmitted her characteristics to her progeny. Thirty years ago this same bitch became the ancestral dam of the Engelmann kennels; and her bloodline has never been deviated from. Even today her blood flows in the veins of the best and most efficient Dachshunds from this kennel, who re-

Jane Castoral bottle-feeds this seventeen-day-old orphan puppy. Mamma was Westphal's Holly, and Dad, Ch. De Sangpur Footloose. Owner Mary Castoral of New York. Photo by Frank Castoral.

ceived the highest awards in dog shows, den trials and field trials. To name only the most famous, there was "Raudel v.S.," "Plus II v.S.," and "Stepke v.S." The latter, the youngest is the best proof, since he received first prize for the most beautiful and keenest Dachshund in a trial according to club rules, and "Excellent" for conformation on dog shows under Dachshund club judges, as well as a "Ia prize" in the den trial of a Dachshund club. The earliest precocity and therefore the strongest inherited tendency was displayed by the deceased "Raudel v.S." When he was $3\frac{1}{2}$ months old, he encountered a very young fox cub in a box. The box was opened and the little "Raudel" just happened to be there. Out of curiosity, he stuck his nose into the box; and jumped back in horror because the little fox had struck at his nose; but immediately he recoiled, entered the box and sank his teeth into the cub. One month later he won first prize in puppy den trials; he choked the fox cub within three minutes. And so he remained all his life; he was very potent in transmitting precocity and assured keenness. His best son for hunting purposes was probably the highly esteemed "Bürschel v. Scharfenstein." He too, was a prepotent sire, a product of inbreeding like "Raudel."

Therefore, if you keep the puppies until they are four or five months old, you can judge their early maturity for hunting purposes and choose accordingly. It is regrettable, that at this age the future stance of the Dachshund, generally, cannot be determined with certainty. In this respect, the critical age is between eight to ten months. Sound judgment in the choice of puppies only comes through practice.

Suppose the breeder was lucky and has kept back for himself the best dog and the best bitch, much will then depend on how they are raised. And that calls for air and sunshine, much work, and exercise, no prison life in the kennel, and wholesome food: veal bones, meat, rice, oatmeal, here and there some milk, as well as all sorts of good table scraps; no seasoning, nothing that is sour or sharp, no fish bones and no poultry bones.

The three main dangers, which lurk in the life of puppies, and especially of those who live in the city, are: first worms, then distemper and last mange. About seventy per cent of all puppies have worms. It can happen that the worms are so numerous that they block the intestines, which can result in cramps and a quick death. If a puppy hedges without reason, and if he has a bloated belly, and loses his playfulness, then one should think immediately of worms and ask a veterinarian for help.

Besides these hazards, buses and especially automobiles take a larger yearly toll than you might suspect. Early training should make sure that the half-grown Dachshunds soon learn to walk on the leash and stay close at the heels in busy streets.

It is not our purpose to go into the health and sickness of a Dachshund here. To "diagnose" sickness by the book is only too often a two-edged

Kühne and Rolly are von Fürstenfels wirehaired Miniature Dachshunds, co-owned by Dr. and Mrs. Wurm of Germany. Photo by Anneliese Wurm.

Playful six weeks old puppies. Co-owners Burt and Pat Kennedy of Pennsylvania. Burt took this picture from above.

Ch. Penthouse Chateau Neuf d'Pape; judge Martha Brandon. Owner-handler Howard Atlee of New York. Photo by Jusinsky.

Ch. Dackelborg's Baby Doll, ML ("Putzi"); judge Wilfred E. Boyer. Owner Edita Van der Lyn of Arkansas; handler Hannelore Heller. Photo by Norton of Kent.

sword; so is particularly the home doctoring out of books or following the well-meant advice of good friends. It is always best to ask a veterinarian early enough.

COMMENTS ON THE DISC PROBLEM*

By Edita Van der Lyn

(Trainer of Dachshunds for TV, stage, and screen, and member of several Dachshund clubs.)

Too much jumping and sitting up—are these to blame for disc problems? They *alone* are not the cause, but disc trouble could occur if one's dog indulges in the above feats indiscriminately. Dachshund owners who pushed toward a lower jump in obedience, know that you cannot ask the same of one Dachshund as you would for others. Individual structure, size and psychological makeup play an integral part in this problem.

The pet Dachshund owner can do much to alleviate potential disc trouble or even prevent it just by using a little common sense. In my act, the first thing that my dogs are taught is to get on to a pedestal (7 inches high) while I set up props and to *remain* there during the performance. This pedestal is home base and, no matter where I am or what the conditions are (people, commotion or noise), they will stay put. This, in itself, is a feat. I utilized this pedestal method into a very practical move at home. I place stools (four sturdy legs with wooden top that is either rubberized or covered with a towel) in strategic areas upon which my "Mexican Jumping Beans" would sit—like certain beds, sofas, settees.

When quite young, I teach them to use this half-way route. Actually, all I do is create a habit. If they forget to use the stool, I simply lift them off the furniture and command them to use the stool. By the way, when a Dachsie gets old and his limbs aren't as lithe as before, he will appreciate the stool.

Once your treasures have been taught to sit and stay on the pedestal, have some fun. By moving the pedestal into the living room when you have guests, you will create a conversation piece—the *pièce de resistance sans pareil!*

It makes sense that jumping onto a soft surface will rarely harm a Dachshund, but the jump down onto a hard floor can and often does. Teach yours to jump both ways via the stool and consider it just another obedience

* *Adapted with permission from* The American Dachshund, *February 1971, pp. 4 and 5.*

exercise. Too many obedience exercises end in the obedience ring when they should be applied to practical everyday situations.

Dachshunds are swimming fools—swimming seals—with the endurance of an otter. One of mine did all his own swimming (and there was lots of it, due to retakes of various actors) when we worked on some of the "Flipper" TV series, while two other smooth Standards acted out different roles as stand-ins. But let me warn any Dachshund owner who thinks it is cute if his Dachshund takes a dive—be it family swimming pool or any other body of water. Never, but *NEVER*, permit your Dachsie to jump from any height into water. The jarring thump is a severe insult to its spine and I know of several tragic disc cases as a result. Lift your Dachshund into the water or let him walk in. Discourage any kind of dives from the very start, and, if at the seaside, beware of the waves—they can drown your Dachshund before your tears start to fall.

Apart from pet owners, kennel owners, too, on occasion, go through the heartbreak of disc trouble. A long back with excessive poundage puts a tremendous strain on the spine. Another theory of mine is that too many of our Dachshunds live sedentary lives. Kennel dogs with adequate runs are more inclined to play and exercise than the solitary pet, unless the owner takes the time and trouble for daily walks.

I think my training experiences prove that too much importance is given to jumping and sitting up as having direct bearing on disc problems. However, every Dachshund is an individual within an individual. Only the owner, through careful observation and common sense, can decide if his half-a-dog-high and two-dogs-long friend should be allowed to "sit up pretty" or leap through hoops like "the man on the flying trapeze."

Temagimi's Dorian going through double hoops on a narrow plank atop stepladders, four feet high. Owned and photographed by Edita Van der Lyn.

Baroness Edita's troupe of nightclub performers include (from left to right): Akita Tani's Aka Kosho; Dondach's Wee Tonic, ML; Ch. Dackelborg's Baby Doll, ML (winner of WB, BW, five points, and BOS at the Western Pa. D.C. and the N.M.D.C. Round-up, Sept. 1970); and Glo-Val's Johann, ML. Owned and photographed by Edita Van der Lyn of Arkansas.

Edita Van der Lyn of Arkansas and her first troupe: A longhaired Miniature Dachshund, three smooth Standard Dachshunds, and one German Shepherd. Photo by Grand Mendoza of Miami.

Akita Tani's Aka Kosho taking Dondach's Wee Tonic ML for a water ride on a lake. Owned and photographed by Edita Van der Lyn.

A CART FOR SMALL DOGS
WITH POSTERIOR PARALYSIS*

Robert L. Leighton, V.M.D.

(School of Veterinary Medicine, University of California, Davis, California.)

For several years there has been increasing interest in the treatment, both surgical and medical, of posterior paralysis caused in the main by ruptured intervertebral discs. Frequently veterinarians are asked to provide some type of cart to enable these patients to move about and exercise more easily. Since the greater number of these patients are relatively small dogs, the cart described here (Figure 1) is quite suitable. It is lightweight, adjustable, serviceable and functional, and it can be constructed of readily available materials (Figure 2).

The wheels, axle and hubcaps are the type used on children's toys. The body-support bracket, sidebars and yoke are made of aluminum rod. The four clamps are called *tiller clamps* because they are used to secure the tiller

* *Reprinted with permission from* Veterinary Medicine/Small Animal Clinician, *June 1966, pp. 554–556.*

Fig. 1. The cart in use by a postsurgical patient. Tiller clamps on the sidebars of the yoke and on the legs of the body-support bracket permit adjustment of height and length of the cart to fit the patient.

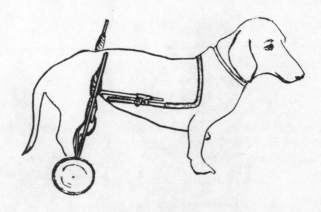

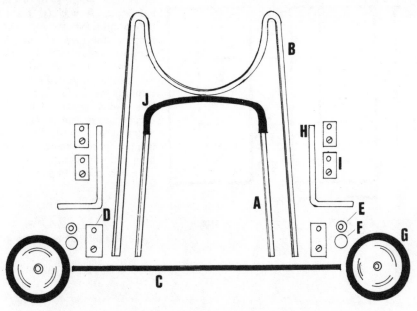

Fig. 2. Material needed for construction of cart.

A—Yoke   D—Axle support   G—Wheel
B—Body-support bracket   E—Washer   H—Sidebar
C—Axle   F—Hub cap   I—Tiller clamp
              J—Rubber-tubing cover on yoke.

or rudder cable in boats. They are heavily galvanized and are supplied with brass tightening screws.

The axle supports (Figure 3) are 2-inch lengths of 1-inch-square aluminum block drilled across the bottom where the axle is inserted, and down from the top to receive the ends of the body-support bracket. Holes are drilled and tapped at right angles to these holes to receive the roundheaded brass screws used to fasten these parts securely. Washers are placed between the wheels and the axle supports.

The curved portion of the body-support bracket is padded in the same manner as a Schroeder-Thomas splint (Figure 4). The yoke is covered with rubber tubing (Figure 5). The tubing will slide onto the aluminum rod more easily if the tubing is moistened.

Dimensions of all parts can be varied to fit the patient.

Although the author receives many requests for information about building these carts he makes no claim for the originality of the design.

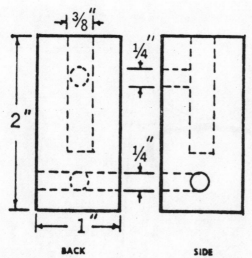

BACK   **SIDE**

The two axle supports are made of 2-inch lengths of 1" x 1" aluminum. A well ($\frac{3}{8}$" diam.) is drilled into the top of each to receive the legs of the body-support bracket. The channel ($\frac{1}{4}$" diam.) through which the axle passes is drilled horizontally through the block near its base. The wells and channels are tapped with holes ($\frac{1}{4}$" diam.) which will receive the round-headed brass screws used to hold the body-support bracket and axle in place.

Fig. 3. Details of axle supports.

Fig. 4. A back view of the cart showing the padding around the body-support bracket.

Fig. 5. A side view of the cart showing the rubber tubing around the yoke.

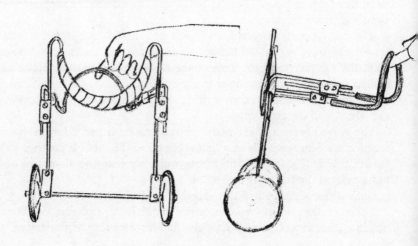

Halian's Damon Flame, at three months rests in the grass with Schuco's "Olympia Dachshund Waldi." Owner Mrs. Hanna Hale of New York. Photo by Dr. Helmut E. Adler.

GENERAL EDUCATION OF THE DACHSHUND

Dachshund puppies should grow up in fresh air. It is considered advisable to housebreak them as early as possible. An unclean and untrained dog in the long run is impossible to stand. Every place one goes with him one creates annoyance. "To the well mannered dog, also a wise man feels congenial." Therefore one should take the young dog into the living room early. First though, teach him to walk on the leash. The first time he will act like a wild dog. He will jerk, jump in all directions, leap, lie down and start wildly up again. By all means go on unconcernedly, pull him gently and evenly along, even when he braces himself with all four legs. Here and there one can stop a little while to praise him, to stroke him, and to offer him a tidbit. Then continue to walk, and so forth. Most often a quarter of an hour's walk is enough to overcome the main difficulties. The next day begin teaching him always to walk on the left side. On the third day one should practice walking around trees and other obstacles. On the fourth day leash him and leave him somewhere for about twenty minutes. There are some clever little fellows who bite the leash off. Such ingenious self help has to be defeated by using a chain.

Whenever the trainee walks well on the leash, start the indoor training. At first get him used to one special place by using the chain. But do not forget the destructive spirit of young dogs; nothing is sacred to them. To distract a puppy from other objects one should give him a big bone, which will keep him very busy.

Now starts a dreary chapter: *housebreaking*. "The one can achieve it

Three generations of Longhaired Miniature Dachshunds: center, De Sangpur Wee Rouge (only Dachshund, all coats, in Philips System Top Producing Dams for 1968), dam of Ch. Patchwork Johnny Come Lately on right, who is sire of Patchwork Antigone on the left. Owner Patricia Beresford Fowler of Virginia. Photo by William P. Gilbert.

Two Wirehaired Standard Dachshunds: left, Ch. Amboss; and puppy, Westphals' Dire Straits on the right. Owner Gerda Statsmann of New York. Photo by Paula Wright.

without any strife, while the other never learns it all his life." Actually there are dogs, who become housebroken almost by themselves. Whereas others can never be taught completely either through kindness or strictness. Luckily this type is in the minority. But a great many make a lot of trouble in any case. At first take the beginner out doors as frequently as possible and also long enough for him to perform. Five minutes is usually not sufficient. If you leave the trainee alone in a room, leash him in the usual place, at least for the first four weeks. While they are on a short leash, dogs do not relieve themselves very readily. Or else, put him in a box or in the familiar travel basket. There, too, he will not like to soil. At night leave the trainee in such a container. Left free in a room, he will, at first, promptly and cheerfully take care of his needs. Then one should take him gently but in a determined manner and push him into his little "calling card," scold him and transport him outside. The speed of this procedure can be increased every day. Some dogs understand the purpose of this routine within a few

Three 'Starry-eyed" Smooth Miniature Dachshunds: from left to right, Ben y Lan Andromache; Ben y Lan Her Wee Grace; and Ch. Ben y Lan Leda M. Co-owners David E. and Raymond C. Thomas of Ohio. Photo by William E. Kelly.

"Easy Rider," un-named puppy of Heidi von Meader's blue litter; owner Pat Kennedy of Pennsylvania. Photo by Burt Kennedy, Jr.

days, while others often do not understand what is wanted of them after weeks of training. Still others grasp it quickly, but falsely. Thus it happened that a gentleman received a half year old Setter. After every "misdeed" the man dipped the Setter's nose into the puddle, etc., clicked his tongue, and then flung him gently out the ground-floor window. For three days the dog pondered in vain. On the fourth day he "caught on." Again he performed his "business" in the room. When his master came home, the Setter greeted him joyfully, then dipped his nose himself into the "calling card" and jumped gracefully out the window.

Communication between man and dog does not work so easily; therefore patience and forebearance are needed. At least half of the thrashings a dog gets dished out belong for his owner. Circumstances, where mutual understanding ceases to exist, are frequent. The inability of the owner to differentiate between the dog's misunderstanding and his unwillingness leads often to repeated trouble and unjust punishment. As soon as a young dog walks about restlessly, searching steadily, and turning around in a circle, then quick action is necessary to shove him out the door; that is, of course, only on the ground-floor; otherwise he has to be taken down to the yard or to the street.

Arty and Yukie of Barqua Kennels, known for their dappled Dachshunds. Co-owners David (shown here) and Mary Bartlett (who took this photo) of Nebraska.

Timettes Red Caprice-M at five months. Co-owners Norman (handler) and Earnestine Walley of Ohio. Mrs. Walley took this photo.

Black Licorice
watches over
children at play.
Owner Mrs.
Hanna Hale of
New York. Photo
by same.

PET THERAPY*

By Boris M. Levinson

Very subtle changes occur in the family constellation when a pet is introduced. This is particularly true in the small family where the symbiotic relationship *(app.: ties; L.L.A.)* between mother and child often needs the kind of redirection accomplished by bringing a pet into the situation. Like a lightning rod, the pet diverts pressure from the child—who then has an opportunity to direct his thoughts outwardly toward his pet. The child also learns that sharing a loved object, a pet, does not mean losing it. Nor does the loved object love one less merely because it also offers its affection to others.

* *Reprinted in part by permission from* Psychological Reports, *1965, 17, 195–198.)*

The three Adler kids: Evy, Barry and Bevy with five Von Hohenhorst puppies. Owner Leonore Loeb Adler of New York. Photo by Dr. Helmut E. Adler.

Mary Minnis giving large dosage of TLC (tender loving care) to eight-week-old Ch. Apollo's Eagle v. Charlynna. Co-owners Charles and Lynn Lanius of Washington. Photo by Lynn Lanius.

Love makes the world go 'round for Beverly Adler, with v. Hohenhorst's Georgie Girl-M (owned by Leonore Loeb Adler). Photo by Stewart G. Daub.

LADIES' DAY—EVERY DAY FOR DACHSHUND OWNERS

During an interview in Germany, the well-known German breeder of wirehaired Dachshunds and expert Dachshund photographer (see photos of whelping series), Dipl. Ing. Rudolf Insam told Stanley Orne, Editor Emeritus of *The American Dachshund* (March 1971, p. 6), that "seldom are good dogs raised in a home or kennel unless both husband and wife are interested."

In order to show that the American ladies are very much "involved," here are some photos to prove this point.

Dot Mullen of Pennsylvania, D.C.A.'s Field Trial Secretary, with her Lorelei of Da-Dor, who has seven and one-third points toward her F.T.Ch. Photo by Howard Morse.

Leonore Loeb Adler, the author, with De Sangpur Wee Bell of the Ball, "Bella," to whom this book is dedicated. Photo by Dr. Helmut E. Adler.

Deanna Kennedy with Middle Creek Suzy of Da-Dor (smooth). Co-owners Burt and Pat Kennedy of Pennsylvania. Photo by Burt Kennedy.

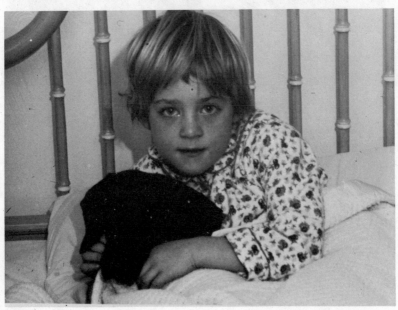

Halian's Damon Flame being hugged by owner Hanna Hale of New York.
Photo by Martin Hale.

Mary Bartlett of Nebraska with her Barqua's Herr Hershey L, a chocolate dappled Dachshund. Photo by David Bartlett.

Batzenhof's Fancy Lotus-Eater ML looks at friend, Wookie, the Citron Crested Cockatoo, held by owner Irma Mickley of Louisiana. Photo by Kurt Mickley.

Ch. Anchor of Heying-Teckel was the last offspring and 95th champion of Ch. Favorite v. Marienlust, pictured celebrating his sixteenth birthday sitting on Mrs. Rose Heying's lap before opening birthday gifts. He was bred by Rose and Fred Heying and bought as a puppy of seven months by Mrs. Ethel B. Bigler of California, who took this picture.

Owner Veda A. Curtis of Alaska is holding two miniatures: left, Kleinen Prinz von Wolfgang; and right, Fraulein Krista Losalinda. Photo by George W. Curtis.

Owner Mary Castoral of New York is pictured relaxing with Torals Stormwarning (on her lap) and Torals Shades of Night. Photo by Frank Castoral.

A happy family group enjoying the affection of their longhaired Standard Dachshund, here are (from left to right) Patricia, Stacey and Sanford Roberts of California.

Beverly and Evelyn Adler dividing their attention between Messrs. Stuart D. Slugh and Scott B. Nelson, and some of the von Hohenhorst Miniature Dachshunds, whose owner is Leonore Loeb Adler. Photo by Dr. Helmut E. Adler.

HINTS ON GROOMING*

By Peggy Aldis Westphal

Director of the National Miniature Dachshund Club; on committees of many Dachshund Clubs, where she is a member. Also a judge, breeder, and handler of renown.)

At Von Westphalen, we have a time table, that is very important in the consistent and correct presentation of show wires. Our time table is based on two things: first, the coat itself and secondly, the dog's ability to replenish his coat after a complete stripping out.

We evaluate a dog's coat at four months, and keep no "fuzzies" or "silkies," since this aspect of wire coats doesn't enter our scheme of things. Is the coat thick with long guard hairs? Or is it very harsh, very flat, very close lying and tight? If it is the latter, very little will ever need to be done. A neatening with trimming shears at the "cowlicks" and tidying up the feet should be sufficient. Now and then, before the coat blows, it may be wise to strip out—especially if one is heading towards a major show. The other type coat (far more common) presents problems, since this coat grows in quicker than the "iron" flat coat—usually six to eight weeks are required, versus the ten to twelve weeks for the "iron" coat.

If you notice, the wild boar individual hair carries three colors—beige, then brown, then either a very dark brown or black. Frequent stripping, tidying up, plucking "here and there," it seems to us, destroys the general crisp outline of a dog—both coat and *color* wise. If a dog is tempered with too much, it looks "muddied"; i.e., the outline is not composed of the darker outer hair color that has been allowed to grow back in, *universally* and *generally* all over the body.

We advocate a complete stripping out almost twice a year. When we say stripping out, we mean to the point where the dog must be protected from the summer sun. Furnishings are left on (they take forever to grow), but to all intents and purposes, the dog's coat is nonexistent. The dog is then shown in its new tight jacket, and can be kept going by "rolling" (partial stripping) for perhaps six months when the cycle is repeated.

The conception that cold dry air induces coat growth is false. Humid warmish air is far more conducive. We keep a washer/drier going in the kennel which aids immeasurably. Toweling with warm damp cloths also helps as does crating a dog in a body heat-retaining aluminum crate.

One other thing. We also clip our retired dogs. Surprisingly, their coats

---

* *The part on the wire coat is adapted by permission from* The American Dachshund *Letter to the Editor, May 1971, p. 9.*

return with the same qualities of the conventionally stripped ones—double, tight and exceedingly presentable. It takes far less time, the dogs look nicer—and can still be headed for a show, if need be, providing a correct estimate of the time required to grow a new coat is heeded.

The grooming of smooths presents no problems. If the dog is healthy, the coat should be sleek and shining. The dog can go into the ring with a "sponge off" of warm water to remove surface dust. Nails and whiskers should be trimmed. Sometimes thick coated smooths can benefit greatly by having the two ridges of hair on the front of the neck trimmed.

Longs, too, if correctly coated (slightly wavy and flat—a "setter" coat) present a minimum of problems. Before showing, bathing is a must. The feet hairs should be kept tightly trimmed, and kept short between the toes and foot pads to emphasize their tightness and neatness. The throat and the area immediately below it should be kept neat and tidied with thinning shears. Taking off this excess coat helps to emphasize the dogs' elegant length of neck.

Sparsely coated dogs should be bathed with good hair shampoo to fluff and give body to the coat—every hair counts!

Dogs with profuse coats that tend to "curl" should be "towelled" after bathing, to flatten the coat over the topline and rib cage.

Ch. Colonel Klink V. Wanderlust is ready to go to the show in his station wagon suite. Owner Eugene H. Shabatura of Minnesota. Photo by Duluth Herald News Tribune.

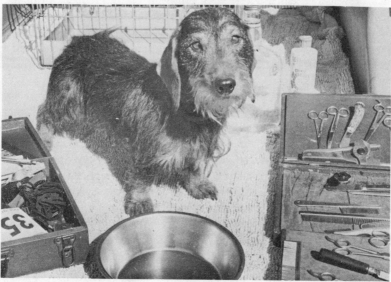

A three months old Tori-Jarice smooth Miniature
Dachshund. Owner Jeanne A. Rice of New York.
Photo by Salvatore Miceli.

Two three-month-old puppies: Smooth, Ch. Von Roblo's Shady Lady;
Longhaired Miniature, Ch. Westphal's Merry Mite. Both owned by Peggy
Westphal of New York. Photo by Allen Westphal.

Ch. Sunara Firecracker with his owner, Mrs. Charlie Mays of California.

KEEPING A STUD DOG

Anyone who has not done some breeding himself should not keep a stud dog for outside use. Those who have not shared the joys and sorrows of the owners of brood bitches, who have to avail themselves of strange stud dogs, cannot sufficiently appreciate their, often justified, concern and worry. "What makes a dog GOOD?

Personality, pedigree and performance."

"What makes a dog GREAT?

ONLY HIS PROGENY!"

So says Mrs. Charlie Mays, owner of Ch. Sunara Firecracker, a longhaired Miniature, who was imported from Great Britain. Accompanying this chapter is a sequence of this little GREAT Stud Dog with his eight champion offspring. (By the time this book is published we may have a number nine since she has six points and is only eight months old.)

If you have decided to offer one or more dogs at stud, first see to it that you have a safe, well closed room for brood bitches sent in to be bred.

The thought and action of the bitch almost always aims at being reunited with her owner. Anyone who cannot take over her care personally, and has no well-trained, efficient help, may, sooner or later, have an unpleasant experience in store. You might as well realize beforehand that the acceptance of strange brood bitches takes a great deal of time, often in no proportion to the usual compensation. Without at least half a dozen letters one cannot come to an agreement with most senders. There are many people who are modest and understanding. Others, though, and unfortunately there are quite a few, are very fussy and, afterward, cannot exhibit enough stupidity and spitefulness. To illustrate: A forestry ranger wrote a breeder that he could not pay the stud fee, and also that he could not give any puppies in return, since all were already promised. The breeder replied by stating that he would let the ranger have stud service for his bitch free of charge, since he was a professional hunter, and so it happened. The bitch was snippy, not at all housebroken, and had to be taken care of by the owner of the stud for

Ch. Mays' Chim Chim Cher-ee ML went to Best of Variety at the Westminster Kennel Club's annual Dog Show in Madison Square Garden, New York, February, 1969, under judge Mrs. Albert E. (Ramona) Van Court. Co-owners Cecil and Olive Callahan of Indiana; handler Hannelore Heller. Photo by Evelyn M. Shafer.

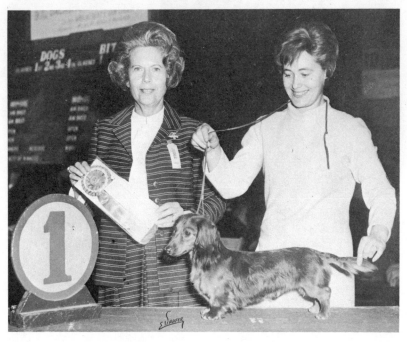

ten days, since she was sent much too early. The bitch was in a continuous excitable state, howling day and night, so that even the neighbors complained. She did not want to eat right and was a great bother. After the mating she was sent home postpaid in a new crate supplied by the breeder (the other one was cruelly small). Everything was in vain. A week later the breeder received a very tactless letter, reproaching him because his bitch arrived in a neglected condition, thinner, and her coat had become worse. She was wirehaired. Later, another nasty card was received: he was very disappointed that his brood bitch had only four puppies, and on top of it all, two were female. The previous time, from another stud dog, she had five puppies of which three were male. After "a year and a day," it was learned from the studbooks, that five offspring were registered out of this bitch showing this breeder's stud dog as the sire! Don't ever believe that this kind of mixture of stupidity and spite is an isolated case. A well-known Dachshund breeder tells of a more incredible story which happened to him. The best of all, though, was a postcard on which he read the following words: "Your cur bred with my bitch in such a way that the puppies had to be delivered by an expensive veterinarian."

A great danger exists in that a strange bitch can introduce distemper and mange. A careful examination of each bitch to be bred is absolutely essential.

Ch. May's Alouette ML (left) pictured at less than three months of age is now owned by Mrs. Leslie A Behm of Wisconsin. Her two other companions are Mays' Tippacanoe MW (center) and Mays' Torino MS (right, both owned by Charlie Mays of California. Photo by Darwin Wilson, freelance photographer for the San Diego Zoo.

Ch. Martinosky's Dresden Doll ML; bred and owned by Ruth Martinosky of California. Photo by Fran Hall

Ch. Martinosky's Shady Lady ML; bred and owned by Ruth Martinosky of California. Photo by Fran Hall.

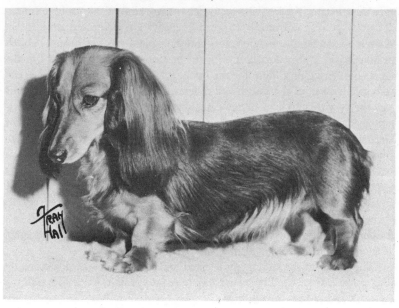

Ch. Ellis Sir Stubby David ML; owner Mr. and Mrs. Robert Ellis of South Carolina.

A bath in a disinfectant before and after mating is advisable, if one has a capable assistant. Bitches who seem to have any kind of skin trouble should definitely be refused, unless a medical certificate is presented stating that there is no danger of contagion. It is always recommended to bring the bitch personally, if at all feasible. It is to the advantage of both parties and the most considerate procedure for the bitch. At the same time, her owner can convince himself of the health and other attributes of the stud dog. In this way the very tedious and, in any case, always insufficient correspondence is not needed. The *"Verein für deutsche Schäferhunde (S.V.)"* ("Club for German Shepherd Dogs (S.V.)") of Munich pioneered with respect to stud dogs in this regard. They brought out a "Selection order" which is strongly recommended by the Dachshund clubs for adoption. The most important points are excerpted here:

"Dogs of more than 20 months of age, will be approved for stud service, if they have proven themselves suitable for breeding. Selection will last for one year only. Therefore the dogs so selected should be inspected again at later selection dates for further approval.

"The owner of the stud dog is obliged to feed and keep the dog correctly (but not in a kennel!). The owner should see to it that the dog gets training for work and is kept in condition. . . .

"Selected dogs must show the German Shepherd dog characteristics and good aptitudes for work.

"The evaluation of the tendencies depends, among other things, on obedience, keenness, and sense of smell.

"Selection should be completely free of any notion of show judgment. Show activities in time will have consequences which will work against the breed: in the potency and transmission which are influenced by the unwholesome moving about from show to show, the unselective preference of show champions, and the race of the buyers for 'champion offspring,' and finally the profiteering.

Ch. Squier's Longfellow V Mays ML; judge Dr. William Houpt. Co-owners Usual and Bernice Squire of California; handler John Davidson. Photo by Bennett Associates.

Ch. Nakamura's Wee Willie wins Hound Group One over 501 other entries at the Santa Clara Valley Kennel Club under judge Howard H. Tyler. Co-owners Paul and Minnie Nakamura of California; handler Jack Cook. Photo by Bill Francis.

Ch. Mays' Maja von Ronneberg captures winners ribbon under judge Theodore E. Gunderson. Owner Laverne Ronneberg of Arizona; handler Judy Webb. Photo by Morry Twomey.

"Actually breeding for working purposes must remain the basis of all progress, and stay the chief aim: the wish to do the most, in order to achieve the possible.

"One could even think it possible for a dog to be approved even without 'known ancestry' because of other valuable characteristics and achievement, for example in the case of a herding dog, or even better of a herding bitch.

"The job of the official selectors makes us the protectors of the state of health and usefulness of our breed, at the threshold of the future of the German Shepherd."

And the Dachshund? . . .

To breeders, who keep stud dogs and who from time to time have surplus dogs to place elsewhere, one can strongly recommend they have some printed material made up to save valuable time, postage, and a lot of annoyance. The following form, for instance, has proved itself:

213

VOM UNTERLAND KENNELS

(Smooth and Wirehaired Dachshunds)

Owner: John Doe, of Anyplace, U.S.A.

I. *Correspondence.* Every day brings so many requests for information in Dachshund matters, that it is almost impossible to answer all of them promptly or even to answer them at all. It is therefore recommended to enclose always a self-addressed postcard or an envelope, as a time saver, for the reply.

II. *Puppy sale.* Considering today's difficulties in breeding, puppies are occasionally for sale; at present no puppies available*. Inquire with breed clubs, which are frequently in a position to recommend puppies, and do not fall for bombastic ads.

III. *Older Dachshunds* are only rarely available. The sales of dogs well trained for hunting, under the ages from three to four years is unthinkable. Dachshunds completely perfect in conformation and achievement do not exist. Inquiries for these, possibly even trained to give tongue at dead game or sure chokers, are useless from the start. The experienced breeder will make less exaggerated demands than the beginner.

IV. *Stud* service is available under the following conditions:

1. Bitches must be healthy and possess a coat in good condition.

2. The owner of the bitch guarantees that neither the bitch nor any of her kennel mates have had distemper or mange during the last three months.

3. The shipping crate should be high enough so that the bitch can stand up in it.

4. It has never happened that a strange bitch has been lost either through death or escape. However no responsibility will be assumed, even though utmost care will be employed.

5. *Stud fee:* The fee is equal to the minimum price of a good puppy*. The amount is to be paid in advance or will be accepted upon collecting the bitch. *The money will be refunded upon receipt of a good puppy*.

6. If the bitch did not conceive, a second service will cost $...* to defray renewed expenses; the same expenses will be charged for bitches sent too late, who no longer accept the stud dog.

7. Mating certificate will be sent immediately, pedigrees only after litter registration.

8. Upon request the kennel will choose the most suitable stud dog.

9. Since not all bitches can be accommodated, it is advisable to make reservations early. Shipment of bitches without previous reservation are not welcome.

Cross out whatever is not applicable.

10. Frequently bitches are shipped too late. It is better to arrive one week too early than one day too late! The bitch will be well taken care of by the thoroughly experienced assistant*. Send bitches only to him: Address:

BUYING AND SELLING

Before buying a Dachshund, be clear about one point: can you raise a puppy well, or would it be better to select an older Dachshund?

Without doubt a home raised puppy is more fun than an older dog, but the raising of puppies also entails much trouble. I only have to mention here the dirt and damage caused by young dogs. Apart from this, a puppy you raise yourself will turn out to be more expensive than a mature dog already fully developed, considering all the risks involved, especially since one never knows how the puppy will develop physically and mentally.

It is best to accept the advice of an expert breeder, if you do not have any personal experience in this respect. Commercial firms sometimes sell tolerably good Dachshunds, most often, though, they offer only average, and frequently bad merchandise. Dachshund clubs are usually in a better

Ch. Klein Felsen V.D. Garten; judge Mrs. Philip Bishop. Co-owners Mr. and Mrs. William E. Shores of Kentucky; handler Mrs. Virginia E. Shores. Photo by Morry Twomey.

Ch. Groville Twister; judge Major Godsol. Co-owned by Gretchen and Andre B. (handling) Felix of Arizona. Photo by John L. Ashby.

position to recommend good dogs at reasonable prices. Even without paying exaggerated prices, you must understand that the keeping of dogs is connected with an extraordinary amount of difficulties and expenses, so that one has to be skeptical about cheap offers.

By all means take a look at the dog before buying; if necessary do not try to avoid a trip. The seller cannot be expected to send a half-grown Dachshund or even a puppy for inspection.

Now a few words about the price. This fluctuates considerably with today's currency so that definite amounts cannot be mentioned. Set a price, which stands in agreement with food prices and the rest of the household expenses. There is a certain type of breeder who even boasts about having set and received an especially high price. These people are not the best promoters of the cause. Especially when they charge a disgracefully high sum to a professional hunter, who does not breed commercially himself, but needs the dog for the best, and for the breed the most useful, purpose: the hunt.

FINDING HOMES FOR DACHSHUNDS

It frequently happens that breeders are more concerned with placing their Dachshund puppies in good homes than in selling them to people whom they do not know. This is the reason why often a "good dog," or one with some minor faults, will be placed in a home as a pet. In this case, the breeder usually asks for a very low price but withholds the A.K.C. registration papers, so that the Dachshund can be neither shown nor bred.

On rare occasions, a situation may arise requiring (mostly due to lack of space) a Dachshund to be "farmed out." This occurs when a stud-dog or a brood bitch, as well as a show dog, is retired. Under these circumstances, no money and no papers are exchanged, but the Dachshund lives with the new family as his or her permanent home.

Jeffrey Lang of California enjoying the companionship of his Dachshund "Brownie," bought without kennel name or A.K.C. papers. Photo by Lang.

WHEN YOUR DOG TRAVELS

By Jeanne A. Rice

(Assistant Secretary of the Dachshund Club of America, Second Vice-President of the National Miniature Dachshund Club.)

When you decide that your dog is going to travel, you want him to be as comfortable and secure as possible. A few simple precautions will assure both and ease your mind.

Whether traveling by car or plane, feed your dog a light meal and offer him water several hours prior to the time of departure. On very hot days you may offer him a small amount of water immediately before departure. If you anticipate the dog becoming ill while traveling, a motion sickness

Tori-Jarice's Wee Kelly ML; judge J. J. Duncan. Owner-handler Jeanne A. Rice of New York. Photo by Ritter.

Canadian and American Ch. Tori Russet Princess; judge Thomas R. Dunk, Jr. Right, owner Thomas J. Rice of New York, father of handler Jeanne Rice, center. Photo by Earl Graham.

medication or light tranquilizer may be administered, but confer with your veterinarian as to the correct dosage.

If the dog will be traveling by car, you can accustom him to the experience by taking him for several short rides prior to your planned trip. A favorite sleeping cushion or blanket, and a few toys will make the dog feel more at home. It is worthwhile to take along a container of water from home, eliminating any digestive upsets due to change in drinking water. While riding in the car, the dog should never be permitted to lean out the car windows. Such a habit may lead to eye and ear injury from dust and debris carried in the wind; and if he should jump, it may cause severe injury or death. The seat belt of the dog world is a wire crate which can be placed on the seat of your car. Such crates, available through your local pet supply dealer, will protect your dog and make your journey more pleasant.

When the dog becomes restless, it is advisable to stop the car and allow him to relieve himself, after ascertaining that his collar and leash are securely fastened.

It is inadvisable to leave your dog alone in a parked car. If you must

At the Miami International Airport, Edita Van der Lyn of Arkansas kisses Dondach's Wee Tonic ML good-bye. (He was personally accompanied by owner's friend and travelled first class as a *passenger!*—Such luxury, of course, becomes a famous night club star!)

do so, insure that the car is in a well shaded area, and the windows are sufficiently ajar to allow adequate ventilation. Do not leash your dog while he is unattended in the car—the leash may become entangled and strangle him if he jumps from seat to seat.

When traveling by air, you may be allowed to take a small dog on board the plane with you; however, this is a matter of individual policy with each airline. Check with the airline of your choice well in advance of your departure, since some lines will permit only one dog in the cabin and it is necessary to have "pet approval" in order to board with your dog. If your dog will not be permitted in the cabin of the plane and must be placed in the cargo section, it is good policy to mark your ticket "traveling with a dog" so that airline personnel are made aware of the situation.

When the dog is to be shipped in the cargo section of the plane, he must be in a sturdy, lightweight crate which has ventilation openings on at least two sides, a leakproof bottom and a door locking mechanism which he cannot open from the inside. The crate should provide enough room for the dog to easily stand up, lie down and turn around. It is wise to line the bottom of the crate with newspaper which will absorb any moisture should the dog become ill or need to relieve himself while in flight. The ventilation openings should be covered with mesh so that flying objects or legs of other traveling animals cannot enter your dog's crate and harm him. There should be mouldings attached to the crate below the ventilation openings to eliminate the possibility of other cargo being packed too closely, thus cutting off the dog's air supply. Do not place toys or other objects in it, for they may prove hazardous to the dog while in transit. Regardless of individual state and country regulations, it is wise to insure that your dog has had all his inoculations, since there may be otters, grizzly bears, monkeys, parrots, cats, raccoons and salamanders as his traveling companions, to mention only a few.

When you will not be traveling with your dog, the required health certificate and record of inoculations in an envelope should be securely attached to the crate. The envelope should bear the name, address and telephone number of the consignee, with an indication to telephone the consignee upon arrival. Secure a dish and some dry food in an insulated bag along with feeding instructions to the crate, in such a manner, permitting attendants to reach them without being bitten or the dog escaping. Insurance is available and advisable. Question the airline regarding insurance for your dog, although most airlines should provide insurance information as a matter of routine.

Whenever possible, arrange for air shipment of your dog on the most direct flight which terminates at the desired destination. This will avoid possible misrouting and unnecessary delays.

DOG SHOWS

One can be for or against dog shows (exhibitions). But even the opponent has to admit that dog shows, even though they may be an evil, are a necessary one. For how can a breeder know whether he is on the right track with his Dachshunds, at least as regards conformation, unless he can be in a position, at dog shows or exhibitions, to compare his dogs with a greater number of others?

What purpose can dog shows have?

1. They serve, as we just said, as a gauge, and a means for comparing of one's own dogs against others. At a show a breeder can best determine how his breeding efforts compare outwardly with those of other kennels. Is he on the right track. And where does he rank?

2. At dog shows he is in the best position to discover the material he likes best for infusion into the bloodlines of his stock, provided that they have already proved themselves on field trials or would do so later on.

3. Dog shows serve to acquaint the general public with a breeder's stock. In this manner they can form their own judgment by personal observation, and may even find that they can profit by it for their own bloodlines.

4. Dog shows are a convenient way to buy and sell dogs, since there is no place where the choice is greater than at a well attended show.

5. These shows serve to help breeders get acquainted and start personal connections, thereby they offer an opportunity for an exchange of ideas, and favor closer cooperation.

6. Exhibitions give an opportunity to earn some laurels; of course, often enough, very cheap ones. And here we come to some of the disadvantages of dog shows. Because of the high awards given to dogs in classes with few entries, and maybe to top it all under a lenient judge, the general public, especially the beginner, may be overimpressed by some of these dogs. And thus, these Dachshunds may actually become harmful to the breed.

7. A great danger for the breed resulting from dog shows lies in the overemphasis on conformation alone. As a supplement, the wise breeder will always insist on achievements in field trials as well, by the dogs with the best conformation. A dog with perfect conformation is not necessarily a well rounded dog, by any means. Aristocratic structure must go together with hunting nobility.

8. For many people, shows and ribbons deteriorate to become an end in themselves. This point of view leads to a dangerous one-sidedness which takes away from the idea of a breed of working dogs.

Reserve Dog (right) and Reserve Bitch (left) under judge Betty Wick are Ch. Doxglen's Roberto of Nikobar, handled by owner Barbara Nichols of California, and Ch. Kashmir of Nikobar, co-owned by Barbara Nichols and Barbara Reidy of Arizona, who is also handling. Photo by Robert J.

9. Dog shows favor, as nothing else, the pernicious commercialism which drives towards the exaggerated interpretation of the purely formal aspects of the breed standard.

10. Dog shows serve the purpose to rouse the interest of the general public in the aims and duties of the breed and therefore draw new working forces from them. Which dogs should be exhibited? Naturally only those who are of value to the breed. The beginner will do well to let an expert evaluate those dogs which he would like to show publicly. Exhibiting today is an expensive affair; and the possible prizes are rarely or never sufficient to make up for the expense of time and money.

Dogs, who are temporarily not in top physical condition are best left at home. Naturally an understanding judge will not hold it against a valiant fighter, if he comes into the ring with a torn ear, or a missing tooth, or a coat still showing marks of work in the field, and which is not exactly sleek and shiny from continuous indulgence on a soft pillow. Dog shows should serve the breed and not find "faults," which were acquired through work;

223

only those shortcomings should be judged as such, which can be transmitted to further generations.

It should be mandatory that a dog arrive in a clean and well-fed condition, though by no means fat.

It is most regrettable that shows are always connected with great dangers for dogs. They help to spread distemper and mange.

If you are serious about breeding and do not have ulterior motives, then you might just as well save the time and money as well as the unnecessary hardships for your dog. Send him to only a few shows, but only those shows where much competition is to be expected and under recognized strict and fair judges. Otherwise, you only fool yourself. Avoid the many unnecessary classes of only minor importance in which there is no keen competition. These classes of minor importance serve frequently only as places of refuge for secondary material, and also to bring entry fees to the show organization.

If at all possible, accompany your dog to the show and handle him yourself. At the same time, compare all the competition objectively and carefully, and try to form an opinion without being prejudiced in favor of your own dog. It is best to take the decision of the judge quietly, even if you have

Ch. De Sangpur Wee Tinka's George; judge Lester R. Fox. Owner-handler Mrs. William (Grace) Burr Hill of Florida. Photo by William P. Gilbert.

a different, maybe even a better one, but possibly also a worse one. Generally judges make their ratings with the best of intentions. You can ask the judge for his reasons later, if you thought his decision was not clear. If he has time, he will give the information readily; and you can only learn from it. Judges are also human and can make a mistake at times. As we have already stressed the breed standard is "laid down" but its interpretation often varies considerably with the various judges, and this is only natural.

DOG SHOWS IN THE UNITED STATES
By Grace B. Hill

(Secretary of D.C.A. since 1954; Treasurer of the N.M.D.C. for the past 11 years; Secretary of the Jacksonville Dog Fanciers Association; Treasurer of the Jacksonville Combined Specialty Clubs.)

Dogs entered in shows are judged mainly on conformity to their breed standard. However, different judges frequently interpret the laid-down rules differently, though each may be equally correct. Therefore, it is necessary for a dog earning his championship to have won under a minimum of three judges and at least three major shows. The shows are designated "major" if a Winner Dog or a Winner Bitch can earn between three to five points at one show. The number of points awarded—though never more than five at one show—depends on the number of competing dogs which have to be beaten in the show ring. For a championship, a dog must have earned at least fifteen points, which have to be approved by the American Kennel Club (A.K.C.).

There are several types of dog shows in the United States. Generally, these dog shows are organized by dog clubs and are held with the approval of, and under the rules and regulations laid down by the A.K.C. The most popular dog shows for amateur spectators are the "All Breed Shows," in which all A.K.C. approved breeds of dogs can be shown. The one hundred and sixteen recognized breeds are divided into six groups: Sporting Group, Hound Group, Working Group, Terrier Group, Toy Group and Non-Sporting Group. Of course, dogs are entered in their own variety and breed, but before they can compete as representative of their group breed they must have won Best of Variety and Best of Breed over all the others in the ring competition. Finally, the first in each group competes for the highest honor, the coveted "Best in Show" prize.

In order to get young dogs, as well as amateur handlers, accustomed to show procedures, the "Match Shows" are ideal. These shows are not point

Ch. Midas' Fancy Decision (Top Longhair in the United States for 1968 and 1969); judge William W. Hackett. Owner Mrs. William Burr Hill of Florida; handler Thomas Okun. Photo by William P. Gilbert.

Ch. Sangpur Lena Von Copano; judge William W. Hackett. Owner Mrs. William Burr Hill of Florida; handler James Swyler. Photo by Earl Graham.

Ch. Penthouse Steuermann; judge Thomas R. Dunk, Jr. Co-owners Mrs. U. Brace of Ontario, Canada and Howard Atlee of New York, who is handling. Photo by William P. Gilbert.

Ch. Amber v. Waldmann (pictured here at six months); judge is Mrs. Houchin, owner-handler Peggy Westphal of New York. Photo by William P. Gilbert.

Ch. Robdachs Tambourine shown winning Best in Match. Handled by co-owner Sanford L. Roberts; other co-owner Patricia A. Roberts of California.

Ch. Von Relgib's Beau Brummell; judge Judy Goulder. Owner Stanley S. Ohland of California; handler Carl Cantrell. Photo by Alfred Stillman.

Ch. Dunkeldorf's Rittmeister; judge Virgil Johnson. Owner-handler Thomas R. Dunk, Jr. Photo by Earl Graham.

shows, but provide a good opportunity to practice handling young dogs—or inexperienced older dogs—and getting them used to facing the competition in the show ring and to behaving calmly and standing still when the judge handles and examines their body-features for conformity to the breed standard.

A third type of dog show is the "Specialty Show," in which dogs of only one breed are entered. A Specialty Show, however, can also be given in conjunction with an All Breed Show, which is sponsored or organized by an All Breed Dog Club. Frequently such Specialty Shows are all day affairs, especially when they are organized by dog clubs with a large membership, such as the Dachshund Club of America, the parent club of the Dachshund breed. One does not have to be a member of the club to enter a dog in any show. The final competition in a Specialty Show is, logically, "Best of Breed."

At all shows in the United States, Dachshunds are divided into the three coat varieties. Occasionally the "Open" classes are divided into "Red" and "Black-and-Tan" Dachshunds. Usually, all colors are shown together in the many classes of the American dog shows with the exception that "Dogs" and "Bitches" are entered separately.

The classes in which dogs may be entered are as follows:
Puppy Dog (Bitch), 6 months and under 9 months
Puppy Dog (Bitch), 9 months and under 12 months
Novice Dog (Bitch)

Ch. Bellisimi v. Westphalen; judge Philip Bishop. Owner-handler Peggy Westphal of New York. Photo by William P. Gilbert.

Ch. Villanol's Rachel; judge Isidore Schoenberg. Co-owners Jean M. Carvill and Faith N. Hoffman; handler Gordon Carvill. Photo by Evelyn M. Shafer.

American Bred Dog (Bitch)
Bred by Exhibitor Dog (Bitch)
Open Dog (Bitch) Miniature
Open Dog (Bitch) Standard
In addition winners of the above classes are judged in competition for:
Winners Dog (Bitch)—This carries points
Best of Winners Dog (Bitch)
Reserve Winners Dog (Bitch)
Specials (or Champions) compete for Best of Variety
Best of Opposite Sex to Best of Variety
Best in all Coats(optional)
Best of Open Miniature (optional)
Best of Breed

231

Col. Wood of the Citadel presents trophy to Ch. Timbar's Sunshine Special under judge Lee E. Murray. Co-owners Diane and David E. Perry; handler Frank McMartha. Photo by Earl Graham.

Best of Opposite Sex to Best of Breed
First in Groups
Best in Show

Placings in each of the classes are rated as: First, Second, Third and Fourth Prize. Each prize receives a different colored ribbon, although frequently money or trophies are also offered.

There is one type of dog show, the "Puppy Sweepstakes," which can only be entered when a puppy is also entered in one of the regular classes. Here, too, the sexes and the three coat varieties are divided. The following classes may be listed, depending on the dog show rules, for a particular sweepstake competition:

(Junior) Puppy (either dogs or bitches) 6 months and under 9 months

(Junior) Puppy (either dogs or bitches) 9 months and under 12 months

or the listings may read:

Junior Puppy (either dogs or bitches) 6 months and under 12 months

Senior Puppy (either dogs or bitches) 12 months and under 18 months

Winners of each class compete for **Best Junior Puppy or Best Senior** for each coat variety. Afterwards, the **Best Puppy** in each coat variety then competes for **Best Junior** and **Senior Puppy in Sweepstakes.**

The monies received for each class are divided according to the following schedule: 40% for first prize; 30% for the second prize; 20% for third prize and 10% for fourth prize. Ribbons and rosettes may be awarded, as well as silver plate trophies, depending on the sponsoring club.

Dog shows are usually arranged so that exhibitors can take in two shows over a weekend. Often, the Saturday and Sunday shows are organized in nearby geographical locations, which do not require too much traveling for the exhibitor. Meeting other breeders and exhibitors regularly at dog shows, luncheons or dinners creates a specially pleasant aspect of the social side of this "show business." It is therefore no surprise that every year more people participate so enthusiastically in American dog shows.

HANDLING

By Hannelore Heller

(Licensed Professional Handler and Member of several Dachshund Clubs.)

Handling is the proper presentation of the dog by the exhibitor for evaluation by the judge. In order to do this, the judge must check the dog's mouth for correct bite, check testicles in males, feel ribbing, keel length, angulation, texture of coat etc., usually done on the table in a Dachshund ring. Movement from front, side and rear must also be evaluated, and so the exhibitor must gait the dog around the ring.

Considering the fact that entries cost from $7.00 to $10.00 (some even more), and remembering that the judge must examine twenty-five dogs an hour—including time for such things as changing classes and picture taking—it stands to reason, that he has only about one-and-a-half to two minutes for each dog. Simple arithmetic tells us that we are paying about $4.00 a minute or $240 an hour to have the dog judged. Therefore, unless a dog is properly presented or handled to show off his virtues, the money is wasted.

RING PROCEDURE

Arrival with spare time before judging is a necessity. The dogs, unless they are experienced show dogs, should have a chance to settle down, be exercised and have their final touch-up grooming done (the actual grooming is, of course, done at home). Some dogs show better and look better if they are given a light meal an hour or so before judging, although the majority are more alert without this feeding. Water intake should be limited to prevent a bloated appearance. When these final preparations have been completed, the dog is ready for the ring except for his lead.

The proper lead is of utmost importance. Its function is solely to control the dog without breaking the outline of his neck. A $\frac{3}{16}$ inch, flat nylon or leathery type show lead, as closely as possible matching the color of the dog, is most widely used in the Dachshund ring. For the high-spirited dog, a fine, metal English-type control collar can be attached to the above-described show lead. A proper fit of this collar is important. The two rings behind the neck must not touch, for if they do, the dog may back out. By the

Ch. Han-Jo's Flaming Flare L.; judge Thirza Hibner. Co-owners Joseph H. and Hannelore Heller (handler) of Illinois. Photo by Alfred Stillman.

Ch. Kemper Dachs Waldemar wins Best of Breed under judge Norman F. Lough; Mr. Charles D. Cline presents trophy. Co-owners Mr. and Mrs. James S. Kemper of Illinois; handler Hannelore Heller. Photo by Alfred Stillman.

same token, the two rings must not be so far apart that they rub against the back of the ears.

The judge must keep to his judging schedule. Anything that delays him may, of course, annoy him. The exhibitor can do much to keep the judging running smoothly by: being at ringside on time, and having his armband before he is due in the ring. He should also watch and listen to the judge so that he knows what is required of him and stay at ringside if he has won his class or has gone second until he is sure he need not go back into the ring. (A booklet on dog show regulations can be obtained from the A.K.C.).

Every judge uses a certain judging pattern in his ring. The wise exhibitor mentally notes this pattern before going into the ring, so he knows what to expect. In most cases, the judge moves the class once or twice around the ring to watch movement and to get an over-all picture of the dogs in the class. Then each dog is set up on the table (occasionally no table is available and the dog is set up on the floor). Each dog is gaited individually. Some judges prefer to gait the dog in a triangle, some use an L-shape, while others require a straight up and down line (see Figs. 1a, b, and c).

Whichever pattern the judge uses, it will be the same for all dogs. Usually the judge wants the second dog to be set up on the table while he moves the first one, and so on down the line. Sometimes, he will use only his hand to

Ch. Fleming's Jelly Julie; judge George C. Spradling. Owner Dr. Fred A. Lawrence of Indiana; handler Hannelore Heller. Photo by Norton of Kent.

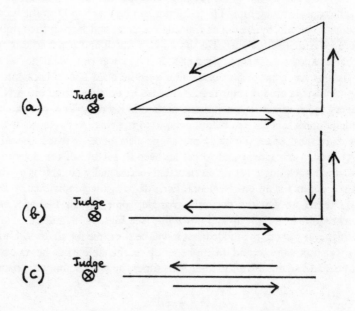

indicate the direction in which he wishes the dog to be moved. Most judges want the dog to stop and stand, without being set up, several feet in front of them as they return to him. The judge may rattle keys or whistle while walking around the dog to see his rear stance (his "outline"). The dog should stand well and look alert. Some handlers use bait in the form of boiled liver, a squeaky toy or anything else that might hold a dog's attention. When the individual examination has been completed, the judge will motion the dog back into line and will often watch the dog move away when the exhibitor thinks he is no longer being judged! When the judge has gone over every dog, he may have all dogs line up in the ring—set up or standing on a loose lead; he may gait the entire class again; he may gait

Westphal's Limerick W. at ten months of age (needing one point toward her championship) is pictured winning WB and BW at Westminster under judge Beatrice Godsol. Co-owners Mr. and Mrs. David A. O'Leary of Illinois; handler Hannelore Heller. Photo by Evelyn M. Shafer.

Fig. 1. Judges' different preferences for gaiting dogs in show ring: (a), triangle; (b), L-shape; and (c), straight up and down.

one or all individually, or he may even move them in pairs—in which case the dogs are side-by-side going away from and returning to the judge.

In the ring the exhibitor may let his dog relax (if this can be done without advertising his shortcomings) while the judge is examining another dog, but the exhibitor must not relax. He must watch the judge and be ready to show off his dog when the judge is looking his way.

During judging, conversation with the judge should be limited to briefly answering a question he may ask . . . Conversations among exhibitors, or with someone at ringside, should be postponed until after the judging. The exhibitor must be courteous to the judge and to the other exhibitors, even if he does not agree with the placement of his dog. Another day—another show. This is a sport and good sportsmanship is in order.

A dog show is a *sporting* event! Exhibitors should dress accordingly. Attire should be sporty and comfortable—not conspicuous. The color of a dress or coat may act as a backdrop for a dog: a black dog set up in front of a navy-blue background will be almost invisible. Shoes should be comfortable and slip-proof. Dangling bracelets, necklaces or belts may frighten or distract dogs.

TRAINING

While there are many ways of show-training a dog, the following is my method. If possible, the show-training should begin when the dog is still a

Ch. Dunkeldorf Richter winning Hound Group under judge Forest Hall. Co-owners Mr. and Mrs. George S. Hendrickson of Illinois; handler Hanne-lore Heller. Photo by Ritter.

Ch. Paradox Festival ML; judge Donia Cline. Co-owners Cecil and Olive Callahan of Indiana; handler Hannelore Heller. Photo by Norton of Kent.

puppy. At first only brush or comb him on the table to familiarize him with it. Encourage him to stand up and then try setting him up, but on no account demand perfection. What is the perfect show pose? Look at the drawing on page 81 of this book. Read your standard. Then go to work, aiming toward these poses.

In front, his legs should be under the body, feet straight forward and elbows close to the body; no daylight visible between the leg and the chest and no toeing in or toeing out. My procedure usually is the following: with the dog's head to my right. I reach over the puppy with my left hand and place that hand under the dog's chest. My right hand is under the neck. I gently raise the front of the dog off the floor or table and then lower it, tilting the dog slightly, so that the left foot touches the platform first. I then let the second foot fall into place. If any further adjustment is necessary, pick up the leg by the forearm—never by the foot—and lift it. Then set it down. Use the left hand for the left leg, the right hand for the right leg in doing this. When the dog's front has been adjusted. I place my right hand under his neck and reach under him with my left hand, sliding it gently

Ch. Apollo's Eagle V. Charlynna; judge Aileen P. C. de Brun. Co-owners Charles and Lynn Lanius of Washington; handler Hannelore Heller. Photo by Morris Photography.

along his underside. I pick up the left hind leg and place it in its proper position. The same is done with the right leg. It sounds simple, but very few dogs will stand in this fashion on the first try. Many a dog, feeling uneasy, will pull back, giving the appearance of a high rear. If this is the case, I pick up the dog and set him up again so that his hind feet are on or near the edge of the table. I now take one hind foot and move it back to let him become aware of the emptiness below him. If that is not sufficient, I place my left hand underneath him taking hold of the left hock and moving both feet off the edge of the table. Then I place them back onto the edge of the table. In most cases, the dog will throw himself forward and thus stand properly. Soon a tug on the tail will suffice in reminding him of that vast drop behind him.

Remember that constant verbal encouragement is necessary. For some dogs a simple "good boy!" is enough. Others need more encouragement. An occasional "stop that!", "steady!" or "stand!" is in order during training then followed by "good dog" when the desired result has been obtained. Don't be rough, but be *firm*. If you are working with a puppy, remember that training should be associated with a happy relationship. A dog without any motivation, working like a robot, is not what we want! A dog wishes to please his master, but he must know what is expected of him.

Now that the front and rear are set up, what next? Try setting him up in front of a mirror. Does he have a level topline or does it sag or roach? If it sags, a little, gentle poke to the underside and subsequent stroking of the side may correct it. If the fearful dog roaches, simply stroking his back may restore self-confidence. If the dog wants to crouch, patiently reset his rear, consistently reassuring him.

Once a dog appears to have learned the basics of being set up, I put a show lead on him to hold his head. Don't worry about the tail unless you have a longhair. Never hold the tail up above the topline. Instead, let it slope down slightly. Opening the dog's mouth frequently and having friends do the same accustoms him to bite examination.

LEASH TRAINING

In most cases, I begin leash training with an English Martingale because the dog cannot back out of it, should he fight the lead. If possible, I take a

Ch. Tallamar's Mistaken Speck MS; judge Mrs. Maitland Satch. Owner Mrs. Leslie A. (Joyce) Behm of Wisconsin; handler Hannelore Heller. Photo by E. H. Frank.

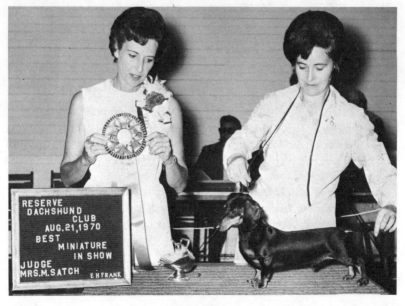

trained dog with an untrained puppy for a few pleasurable walks, stopping to let children, bicycles and traffic pass, reassuring or sometimes scolding as is deemed necessary. The next time, I take the puppy alone and we begin to "work." With the puppy on my left side, I start walking. I never pull on the lead, but give quick jerks with immediate releases, saying something like "come on, let's go" or "that's a good dog!" When I put some enthusiasm into my voice and convey the attitude that this will be fun, he usually perks up. If he leaps forward, I jerk him back or jerk him forward if he lags. If he balks, I keep on walking giving little, sharp jerks on the lead. I am generous with praise, even if he walks only three steps. It is important to enjoy him and let him feel this. When I find my patience giving out, I quit for a while and try not to lose my temper. If he wants to "vacuum the ground," I jerk the lead up. The ultimate goal should be to have him walk on the left side or a little ahead and not too close, with just the slightest pressure on his neck, but also turning corners easily. I teach the dog to walk on my right side as well as on the left, since, when gaiting or setting up the dog, it is well to remember that the judge cannot see the dog if the exhibitor is between them.

Usually many kennel clubs offer excellent conformation classes which also simulate the atmosphere of the show ring. Good practice is further offered at fun matches.

JUNIOR HANDLING

By George C. Wanner

(Breed Judge; Field Trial Judge; Director of D.C.A., D.C.N.J., and Sussex Hills K.C.; D.C.A.'s Delegate to A.K.C.; Chairman of D.C.A.'s Committee on Junior Handling.)

Junior Handling is for boys and girls 10 through 16 years of age.

Prior to April 1, 1971, Junior Handling was set up at each show according to the desires of the local show-giving club. The sole applying American Kennel Club rule was that only Licensed Handlers could judge these classes at an A.K.C. point show.

After April 1, 1971, the new rules and regulations of the A.K.C. were applied stipulating that any judge or licensed handler may judge, but is subject to all restrictions and when judging is not permitted to show a dog at that show.

Classes are divided: Novice—for boys and girls 10 and under 17 years of age who have not placed first in a Novice Class before, and Open—for boys and girls 10 and under 17 years of age who have placed first in Novice

Ch. Wanner's Rusty Wire; judge Alice Marie Cornet. Owner-handler
George C. Wanner of New Jersey. Photo by Evelyn M. Shafer.

at that show or at an earlier show. These two classes may be sub-divided
into Junior, 10 and under 13, and Senior, 13 and under 17 years of age, and
if so desired by the show-giving club, they may be further sub-divided into
Boys and Girls.

The dog handled must be entered for that show and must be owned by
the Junior or by a member of the Junior's immediate family (Father, Mother,
Brother, Sister, Aunt, Uncle, Grandfather or Grandmother). This rule
was generally considered as part of the requirements in the past, but was
broken nearly as often as it was followed. With the new requirement that
an entry form be separately filled out front and back by the Junior Handler,
the ownership requirement will now be fulfilled. It is now very easy for the
A.K.C. to check the ownership of the dog, since the form must be sent in
before show entries close.

The Judging Program stipulates ring and time for judging of Junior
Classes, eliminating the old time wait till about 4 or 5 P.M. for a ring to
open. The catalog will now have a section listing competitors in Junior
Classes.

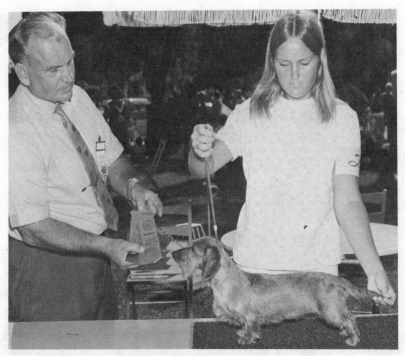

Ch. Wilheen's Little Desiree MW; judge Joseph Kulper. Co-owners Dr. and Mrs. William C. Adams of California, handler Debbie Adams. Photo by Alfred Stillman.

All prizes must be offered as outright awards. No Challenge Trophies for Junior Showmanship! No prizes may be awarded in the ring at a show for one breed of dog being handled, such as Best Junior Handler showing a Dachshund. Therefore, the D.C.A. prizes—authorized at our 1971 meeting for annual award to the best Boy and Girl Junior Handlers handling Dachshunds—will be presented at the next annual meeting.

All this Junior Activity during the year is due to the qualifications necessary for the competition at the Westminster Kennel Club Show in New York's Madison Square Garden in February of each year, where the competition for the Leonard Brumby, Sr. Trophy is held. The A.K.C. Regulations—Section 14 and Section 15—applying to Limited Classes apply to this competition.

The kennel clubs support this activity to interest boys and girls in the showing of pure-bred dogs in a sporting manner. Good sportsmanship, the ability to win and lose gracefully without undue enthusiasm or dismay

Ch. Can Dach's Eric Again CD; judge Thirza Hibner. Co-owners Mr. and Mrs. Frederick L. Kelly of Texas; handler Fred Kelly III. Photo Morry Twomey.

Ch. Vantebe's Krista v. Lucky, winner of Veteran's Class at ten years of age; judge Donia Cline. Co-owners David and Diane Perry of Georgia; handler Greg Perry. Photo by Earl Graham.

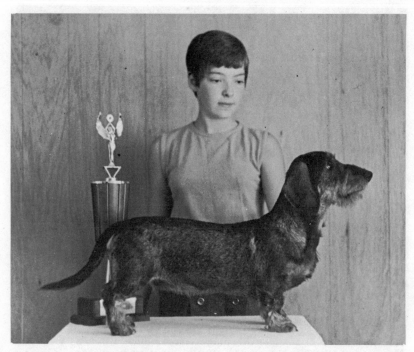

Ch. Stadtwald's Jim Dandy Wire. Handler Elaine Pillsbury, the daughter of co-owners Alice and Dean Pillsbury of Massachusetts.

as the case may be, is a hard lesson to learn, but is frequently demonstrated in Junior Showmanship Classes with an élan that their seniors could do well to emulate. My advice to mother and father is to let your child progress on his own with your encouragement, of course. Show your own good sportsmanship by refraining from publicly commenting on the judging and by privately criticizing your child's performance if you must do so at all.

My advice to Juniors with Dachshunds is, "Don't get discouraged." Dachsies are small dogs and may get lost in classes of twenty or thirty large dogs, but consistent good handling can't be ignored for long. Juniors, with Dachshunds, have gone to the top at the Garden. So show your Dachshunds, have fun and good luck!

Chapter V
The Dachshund and the Hunt

Take the hunt away from the Dachshund—and you take away the roots of his strength; he sinks down to be nothing but a dog.

OBEDIENCE

By Arnold L. Korn, O.D.

(A.K.C. Tracking Judge, Field Representative, National Association of Dog Obedience Instructors, Member of Advisory Board, and Instructor Memphis Obedience Training Club, Former President of the Memphis Dachshund Club, Member of the National Miniature Dachshund Club.)

"Obedience trials are a sport and all participants should be guided by the principles of good sportsmanship both in and outside of the ring. The purpose of obedience trials is to demonstrate the usefulness of the pure-bred dog as a companion of man, not merely the dog's ability to follow specified routines in the obedience ring—the basic objective of obedience trials is to produce dogs that have been trained and conditioned always to behave in the home, in public places, and in the presence of other dogs, in a manner that will reflect credit on the sport of obedience. However, it is also essential that the dog demonstrate willingness and enjoyment of its work, and smoothness and naturalness of the part of the handler are to be preferred to a performance based on military precision and peremptory commands."

The above is quoted from the introduction to A.K.C.'s Obedience Regulations and it is to be hoped that all exhibitors take it to heart.

A dog may successively earn the degrees of Companion Dog (C.D.), Companion Dog Excellent (C.D.X.), Utility Dog (U.D.) and Tracking Dog (T.D.) or when combined with U.D., Utility Dog Tracker (U.D.T.).

OBEDIENCE TRIALS

Obedience Trials are held by a few specialty clubs, by all-breed obedience clubs and in conjunction with specialty and all breed conformation shows. Listings of the dates of these events are to be found in the American Kennel Gazette and in various dog magazines.

Training for these degrees can be done at home with the aid of several of the good books on obedience training, or in classes held by the various clubs and trainers throughout the country. The American Kennel Club would probably have a list of the clubs in your area.

The requirements for the various degrees are fully explained in the pamphlet "Obedience Regulations" published by A.K.C.—single copies, free. To earn the C.D. degree, a dog must earn 170 points of a possible 200 with at least 50% of the available points in each exercise, at three separate trials under three different judges. The same is true for the C.D.X. and U.D. degrees. To earn a "T," the dog must follow a track of between 440 and 500 yards in length laid by a stranger, and find a glove or wallet dropped by the tracklayer. The scent must be at least thirty minutes and not more

Utz von der Traben, UDT, is the first Miniature Dachshund to earn all four Obedience Degrees. Co-owners Dr. and Mrs. Arnold L. Korn of Tennessee. Photo by Warren Studio.

Utz von der Traben, UDT, retrieving over High Jump, 12 inches under "old rules". Co-owners Dr. and Mrs. Arnold L. Korn of Tennessee. Photo by C. E. "Jack" Herndon.

than two hours old when the dog is started. A tracking test is judged by two judges, and must only be passed once in order to win the title.

NOVICE EXERCISES

The Novice Exercises for the C.D. degree consist of heeling on lead, including the figure eight, a stand for examination, heeling off lead, the recall and the long sit and long down.

The *heeling exercises* are judged on the accuracy of the dog staying in the heel position, alongside the handlers left leg, throughout a series of starts, stops, turns and changes of pace, both fast and slow.

On the *stand for examination,* the dog is posed, off lead, and left by the handler who walks about six feet away and turns and faces his dog, while the judge touches the dog on the head, shoulders and hindquarters, and then orders the handler back to his dog. The dog must stand still until re-

Retrieving over the High Jump by three of Dr. and Mrs. Korn's obedience trained Miniature Dachshund: top, Sassy; center, Schlitz; and bottom, Meister. Photos by Dr. Korn.

Utz von der Traben, UDT, jumping the Broad Jump, twenty-four inches at that time. Co-owners Dr. and Mrs. Arnold L. Korn of Tennessee. Photo by C. E. "Jack" Herndon.

leased by his handler, after the judge says, "Exercise finished." The dog must show no fear or resentment while being examined.

On the *off lead heeling*, the dog must go through the same series of starts, stops, slow, fast, left, right and about turns as in the first exercise.

On the *recall*, the dog is left sitting at one end of the ring while the handler leaves him at the judge's command and goes to the other end of the ring and turns to face him; then at the judge's order calls his dog. The dog must proceed promptly at a brisk pace to his handler and sit in front of him, and then when told by the judge, the handler orders him to the heel position.

The *long sit* and *long down* are group exercises . . . the dogs are divided into groups of not less than six nor more than fifteen, and placed in the sit position, and must stay sitting where left by the handler for a period of one minute while the handler is standing across the ring. The dog must not move until released from the exercise after the handler has returned to the heel position. The long down is performed in the same manner, except the dog is left in the down position for a period of three minutes, while the handler is across the ring. The dog must not get up, nor move from his position until released from the exercise.

The maximum number of points available are as follows:

Heel on Leash	35 points
Stand for Examination	30 points
Heel Free	45 points
Recall	30 points
Long Sit	30 points
Long Down	30 points
Maximum Total Score	200 points

OPEN EXERCISES

The Open Exercises for the C.D.X. degree are as follows: heel free; drop on recall; retrieve on flat; retrieve over high jump; broad jump; long sit and long down.

For the *heel free*, as in the novice class, the figure eight is performed also off leash.

For the *drop on recall*, the dog is required to drop to the floor on command or signal from his handler while on the way in, and then on command from his handler, come to sit in front.

For the *retrieve on flat*, the dog is required to retrieve a wooden dumbbell on command from his handler and to return it to his handler, holding it until ordered to "give," and then return to the heel position on command. During the *retrieve over the high jump*, the dog is required to retrieve on command going and coming over a hurdle—the height for Dachshunds being equal to the height of the dog at the withers, or a minimum of eight inches.

For the *broad jump*, the dog is required to jump on command over a series of low hurdles—twice the distance required for the high jump—and to come around to sit in front of the handler.

The *long sit* and *long down* exercise are for three and five minutes respectively, and, in open, are done with the handler out of sight.

Maximum scores for Open are:

Heel Free	40 points
Drop on Recall	30 points
Retrieve on Flat	25 points
Retrieve over High Jump	35 points
Broad Jump	20 points
Long Sit	25 points
Long Down	25 points
Maximum Total Score	200 points

UTILITY EXERCISES

The Utility Exercises are: scent discrimination (articles 1 and 2); directed retrieve; signal exercise; directed jumping and group examination.

To begin the *scent discrimination*, the handler supplies five each of metal and leather numbered articles to the judge. The judge picks one leather article and one metal article, and the balance of the articles are put out in the ring approximately six inches apart and about fifteen feet from the dog and handler. The handler then puts his scent on one of the two articles, with his hands and the judge puts the article out amongst the other eight. The dog and handler face away from the articles, and on the judge's command,

Broad Jump. Dr. and Mrs. Korn's obedience trained Miniature Dachshund: top, Sassy; and bottom, Meister. Photos by Dr. Korn.

the handler sends the dog to find the scented article. The same is done with the other remaining article.

Similarly for the *directed retrieve*, the handler supplies the judge with three white cotton work gloves. While the dog and handler stand in the center of the ring, the judge places one glove to the right of one in the center and one to the left, three feet in from the edge, and three feet from the back of the ring. The judge directs the handler to send his dog for one of the gloves. The handler must turn to face the glove and then command and/or signal his dog to retrieve the proper glove. The dog must go directly to the proper glove and bring it back to his handler sitting straight in front of him.

In performing the *signal exercise*, the dog must go through heeling exercises completely on signal. Then, on the judge's command to the handler, the dog stands on signal and stays while the handler goes to the opposite end of the ring. Then upon signaling, the dog must go down, sit, and come and go to heel position.

In *directed jumping*, the dog must on command go to the opposite end of the ring between a solid jump and a bar jump set up about 18 feet apart, half the distance to the opposite end of the ring. On the judge's order, the handler signals the dog to jump the proper jump and return to the handler. This is done once for the high jump and once for the bar jump.

For *group examination*, the dogs are stood in a group in ring center and left standing, while the handlers leave and stand facing them from the opposite side of the ring. The judge then examines each dog the way they might be examined in the breed ring. The dog must stay in position and show neither fear nor resentment, until the group examinations are completed and the handlers are ordered back to position.

The maximum scores for Utility are:

Scent Discrimination Art. 1	30 points
Scent Discrimination Art. 2	30 points
Directed Retrieve	30 points
Signal Exercise	35 points
Directed Jumping	40 points
Group Examination	35 points
Maximum Total Score	200 points

TRACKING TEST

At a Tracking Test, a dog must be able to follow the track of a stranger for a minimum of 440 yards, and up to a maximum of 500 yards with the track being at least thirty minutes old and not more than two hours old. To enter a Tracking Test, a dog must be certified as ready to be entered in a Tracking Test by a person eligible to judge A.K.C. tracking tests. To earn a "T," the dog must pass one Tracking Test, judged by two licensed judges.

K-Dachs Midnight Sassy, MW and CDX, going over the Bar Jump in Utility. Co-owners Dr. and Mrs. Korn. Photo by Dr. Korn.

Group Performance by the Korns' Mini Dachshunds. Photo by Dr. Korn.

HOW TO TRAIN FOR OBEDIENCE TRIALS

At a recent Obedience Trial, while I was talking to one of the judges during the lunch break, a man walked up and asked him if he was Mr. So and So. This man stated, "I've been to a lot of shows in the past year, and I'm training a dog myself, but I haven't shown him yet, and I disagree with your judging." He went on to call off a number of points, which the judge quickly showed him were correctly judged according to A.K.C. Rules for Obedience Trials. After about five minutes of this man's show of ignorance, the judge asked him if he had ever read the rules, and was told that the man had a rule book, but had not as yet had time to read it. Lesson: *Read the rules* and then *discuss* them with someone who knows what they mean, so you don't make a fool of yourself!

The *age to start training* is a matter of great dispute. It depends on the individual dog and the training class instructor. Generally a six months old puppy can be trained quite well, though some are quite puppyish and care is needed not to be too harsh and create a lot of resentment, to training, the leash, and everything concerned with training. There are some classes taught according to Milo and Margaret Pearsall's "KPT" kindergarten puppy training, with puppies starting as early as three months . . . but this is not formal obedience, just basic training, and with the proper guidance, quite successful, and very rewarding. It is NOT to be experimented with by the Novice.

LEASH BREAKING

One of the best ways to Leash Break a dog is to start out by putting a small leather buckle collar around the puppy's neck several times a day for a short time while praising and playing with him, until he doesn't pay any attention to the collar. Initially many of the pups will try to back out of it or fight it— never allow the pup to get frantic about something like that—just pet and calm him and, if need be, take the collar off, putting it back on a short time later. After the dog becomes used to the collar, tie a short length of light cord or part of an old leash to the collar; by short is meant long enough to drag on the floor but not longer than the dog itself. Stay close enough to the dog so that he does not snag this "leash" on any furniture, or shrubbery if outside . . . again play with the dog and give him plenty of praise while he is wearing this contraption. After he has become used to this, attach a light lead to the collar allowing him to lead you wherever he wishes, while talking and praising him. When he has *BECOME ACCUSTOMED TO YOU* being on the other end of the leash you can start coaxing him to come your way. After he is leash broken you can graduate to the training collar of chain link, nylon, or leather.

TRAINING COLLAR

Proper use. The training collar or "choke chain" is *not* to be used to choke the dog; used properly, it lets the dog know when he is wrong. As the illustration shows, there is a right and a wrong way to put the collar on the dog. Used correctly, the collar tightens and releases, put on incorrectly, the collar does not release and defeats its purpose. A quick jerk and release of the leash will jar the dog, make him uncomfortable and put him off balance, three things he does not like. It doesn't take him long to find out that being in the proper place brings praise and getting in the wrong place makes him uncomfortable.

Proper fitting. The training collar should be the smallest collar that can go over the dog's ears. If you decide to use a chain link collar, have a jeweler remove the extra links, and then resolder the end ring in place. The proper way to measure for a collar is to take a tape measure and loop it over the dog's ears, sliding it back and forth over his head until you find the smallest loop that will fit over his head. This measurement transferred to the collar includes the length of the collar plus the diameter of *one* ring. (See Fig. 1).

THE SIT, THE STAND AND THE DOWN

It has been proven that the best way to train a dog for this is to start when he is young. With your Dachsie on your left side, sit or kneel next to him with your right hand through his training collar, palm down fingers toward the head. With your left hand also palm down on his back, tell the dog to **SIT**, in a firm but friendly tone. As you tell him to sit, slide your hand backwards cupping it around his hindquarters while at the same time exerting backward pressure on his collar to ease him into sitting position. As soon as he is sitting, praise him to the skies, hold him there for a few seconds and then let him up.

Then from a sitting position, tell him to **STAND**, reversing your procedure, by pulling forward on the collar with your right hand and using the left hand to hold his back feet from going forward—the back of your hand under his stomach and the edge of your hand in front of his hind legs, if necessary.

For the **DOWN**, put your dog in a sitting position on your left side, your left hand and arm across his back. With your right hand lift his right foreleg from the floor several times, then do the same with your left hand and his left foreleg, then when there is no resistance to this, raise both forelegs from the ground several times. Eventually raise both forelegs at the same time and ease him forward and down using the weight of your left arm, if needed. Be very gentle so as not to scare the dog.

After the dog is used to being made to sit, stand and go down . . . be sure to use the command **SIT**, **STAND** and **DOWN** each time you do this. Tell him to **STAY** for each of these positions . . . do not allow him to fidget and squirm. Start by making him stay still for just a few seconds and gradually lengthen this until he will sit still for one minute and do the down stay for three minutes. The best correction is a sharp **"NO"**, while putting him back in position.

THE FIGURE EIGHT

The Figure Eight is a seemingly simple exercise performed on leash in the Novice classes, and performed off leash in the Open classes. A lot of

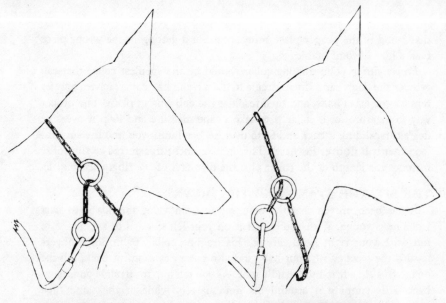

INCORRECT   CORRECT

Fig. 1. Training Collar

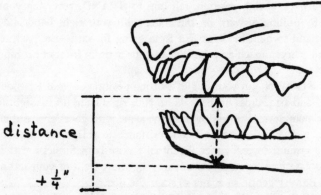

distance

$+ \frac{1}{4}''$

Fig. 2. Measure this distance, and, for clearance, add quarter inch, to allow dog to pick up dumbbell.

Width of mouth means width at point where dog likes to carry dumbbell. Most dogs will carry it just behind canine teeth, but a few prefer to carry it with their molars, which calls for a much wider measurement. The size of the bar, is measured by taking a series of dowels from quarter inch diameter on up, and gently putting it in the dog's mouth, and getting him to hold it till you find the one that fits best. A bar that is too small will "rattle" between his teeth; and one that is too large will force his tongue back in his throat. Fitting the dowel will take a lot of patience with some dogs, but it is worth it in the long run, as this type of dumbbell makes the retrieving exercise easier to teach. After the dog has learned to retrieve, a meticulously fitted dumbbell is not necessary.

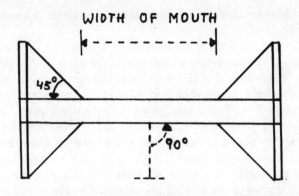

Fig. 3. Dumbbell.

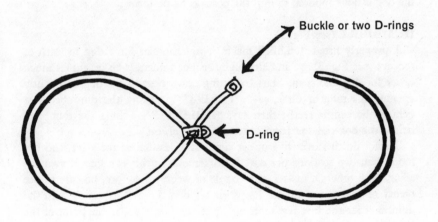

Fig. 4. Figure eight tracking harness.

The best tracking leads are made of diamond braid polypropylene, sometimes used as ski rope. They are lightweight, do not tangle, knot or snag,
and do not absorb water. The harness should be made of latigo leather.

points are needlessly lost in this easy exercise because it is not performed properly. The purpose of this exercise is to demonstrate the dog's adaptation to the handler's pace.

Two ring stewards stand approximately eight feet apart while the dog and handler heel in a figure of eight pattern around these two posts to the judge's command. When the dog is on the inside of the turn he must slow down, and when the dog is on the outside of the turn, he must speed up to keep in heel position. The handler is supposed to keep a steady pace.

Unfortunately, some handlers think they can fool the judge by slowing down when they are on the inside and by speeding up when they are on the outside. However, the judge is watching the feet of both handler and dog, and if the dog does not accelerate when he is on the outside of a turn, he is either lagging or the handler has adapted his pace to the dog . . . a more serious error. The same is true when the dog is on the inside of the turn . . . he should be slowing down, and if he doesn't, the handler has either quickened his pace or the dog has forged ahead . . . either of which is very noticeable from the judge's position in the ring. A further caution . . . the dog is not supposed to *sniff* the posts as he performs.

DUMMBELL (see Fig. 2)

A properly fitted dumbbell makes it much easier for a dog to learn to retrieve (see Fig. 3) . . . and although it is not a must, it makes things much easier for dog and man. Start by sitting down next to the dog and gently opening his mouth. First, say, **"TAKE IT"**, putting the dumbbell just behind the canine teeth; then say, **"HOLD IT"** grabbing the dumbbell before the dog can spit it out, then *plenty of praise.*

Do not do this over five or six times at a session, at the start, and not more than two sessions per day. With some dogs this is a long drawn out affair, with others a matter of a couple of weeks, therefore, be sure to use plenty of praise, and do *not* lose your temper. To make the dog hold the dumbbell for the first few moments, put one finger under the point of the chin on the triangular soft spot exerting a slight upward pressure. Never squeeze the jaws shut on the dumbbell, for this is not only most painful, and can cause much resentment, but it can also set the whole project back for a long, long time.

Our first Dachshund, Edd's Tinker Bell, C.D., was forced to take the dumbbell by an instructor many years ago; consequently, she would run and hide when she saw one. We tried everything, including making a dumbbell whose bar was a chew stick with ends made to slide on. Tinker would hold the chew stick, but if the ends were replaced while she was holding it, she'd spit it out and run. Convinced that somewhere something was wrong, we tried the soft approach with Tinker's pup, K-Dachs Schoshund Madchen, UDT. Madchen would retrieve a rubber dumbbell any place in the back yard . . . but if a wooden one was thrown she'd run out to it, and come back without it to tell you, you had thrown the wrong one. After eight weeks of work for a few minutes every night, she missed but one retrieve in the next six years of showing.

The first sign of progress is when the dog will hold the dumbbell without aid . . . the second sign is when the dog will reach forward the least bit to take the dumbbell . . . the third big step is when he reaches down to take the dumbbell. Finally when he reaches down and forward to take it, and then steps forward one or two steps, you can toss the dumbbell a few feet away, and after that it will be just a few days before your pup will retrieve at any distance.

RETRIEVING OVER THE HIGH JUMP

After your dog retrieves on flat ground, retrieving over the high jump is easy. First, put the dog on leash, and heel over a *low* board (four to six inches). Be sure that your left foot goes over the jump at the same time your dog does, while at the same time giving the command **"jump"** or **"over"**. In the next step, approach the jump but do not go completely over the jump as before, just your left foot goes over as the dog jumps. Then you pull your left foot back and call the dog back to you.

When the dog does this without refusing the jump, you can start retrieving over the same **low** jump. If the jump is kept low enough for him to see over, and done often enough until he gets used to jumping back and forth, you will have a dog that will almost never run around a high jump. Do not raise the height of the jump until he will retrieve from all angles and come back over the jump . . . then you can gradually raise the height to whatever is required by the rules. (Height of the dog at the withers for Dachshunds—minimum eight inches).

THE BROAD JUMP

The dog is required to jump *twice* the distance required for the high jump, or a minimum of 16 inches for Dachshunds. We have taught ours first to jump one hurdle. With the ones that liked to step on the board as they jump, we propped the hurdle at an angle, or even on edge until they get the idea of what is required. We then go to two boards. I have one set of practice jumps made out of $\frac{1}{4}$-inch plywood (for lightness) and the second hurdle has been sawed in half to make two 4-inch sections, so that the progression from eight inches to sixteen inches can be made in two steps.

Care must be taken in teaching broad jump not to *jerk* the dog over the hurdles, for that is a great way to make him hate the exercise! It is almost impossible to jerk the leash without throwing the dog off balance and possibly taking the chance of the dog hurting himself on landing. Try getting him to "heel" over the jump with you, as you hop over it to give him the idea.

After the dog understands what is wanted of him, leave him at a sit stay facing the jump, as you jump over it yourself. Turning to face him, call him to you. As he approaches the hurdle, say, **"JUMP"** and let him come and sit at your feet. After the dog can do this, go back around to the side of the jump as he goes over, so that he will make a half-circle to come to you. Do NOT do this finish every time your dog comes in, as he will get in the habit of doing it, anticipating your command, and finish on his own without coming in to sit in front of you as is required by the rules.

Another way to discourage a dog from stepping on a hurdle is to balance it on a broomstick, or similar object, so that it will provide an unsteady footing for the dog. Screen wire atop the hurdles can be used to prevent the dog from stepping between the hurdles. Each dog has his own preference on the distance he needs for his take-off, find it and use it! We have one seven-and-a-half pound Miniature Dachshund that just likes to take about two steps before jumping her 16 inches.

SIT STAY AND DOWN STAY

For the Novice Exercises the dog must sit stay for one minute, while the handlers stand across the ring facing the dogs; the down stay is for three minutes while the handlers again face the dogs. Dogs must stay in position until the judge says, "Exercise Finished."

In Open, the sit stay is for three minutes, and the down stay for five minutes, while the handler is out of sight. Ideally, these are exercises that should be practised in groups to acquaint the dogs with show conditions. Actually, the basic part of the exercise is to train your dog **NOT** to **MOVE** for the required length of time (one and three minutes for Novice, three and five minutes for Open). Fortunately, dogs have a built-in alarm clock enabling them to time for themselves, therefore, if we insist on NO movement for those periods, they will learn to do the "stays" with no trouble.

TRACKING TRAINING

This is that part of obedience training that I consider the most fascinating. It is hard to understand why more "Dachsies" do not earn the coveted "T" each year. We talked about training "Meister" (Utz von der Traben, U.D.T.) for tracking for about two years, before he ever got out in the field. We wondered if a Miniature Dachshund could go where a Shepherd or Doberman could go . . . we found out real soon, and the answer was an emphatic YES.

We attended a Pearsall instructors' clinic at which the last day was devoted to tracking, that was the start of Meister and Madchen (K-Dachs Schoshund Madchen, U.D.T.) in the field of Tracking. We started making their harnesses (see Fig. 4), and on the Fourth of July week-end we started serious work. In October, Meister became the first U.D.T. Miniature Dachshund, and although Madchen failed her first Tracking Test that same day, she earned her T two weeks later.

We are indebted to our Training Director, Bob Hoisington, for the many hours he spent with us and to Judge Morris Rosenberg for the numerous trips to get certified. They were also in the process of training two German Shepherd puppies to track, and Mr. Rosenberg's Hilde earned her T at the age of six months and one week.

Begin preparing the track for training by spacing two flags about thirty feet apart, heading into the wind, and laying a heavy track between them by scuffing your feet through the grass, keeping in as straight a line as possible. Then throw a leather glove a short distance down the path and get your dog to retrieve it . . . if your dog won't retrieve, you have an additional problem, the easiest way it can be solved is if you can teach your dog to retrieve. The use of food for bait is not the best way to train him, because if your dog is not hungry, he'll not work. Try using the dumbbell method described earlier.

After the dog has retrieved the glove a couple of times, make him stay at the starting flag, while you go out on the track and let him see you drop the glove. Having done this, run back to him and command him to **FETCH**. After repeating this procedure a few times, go out farther but this time do not let him see you drop the glove, and then send him after it. This time he'll have to hunt, and by using his nose to do the hunting, he'll be doing what comes naturally . . . it shouldn't take him long to realize that this is what you have been trying to get him to do. Remember to lavish praise on him each time that he does get the glove, thereby, encouraging him to hunt for it each time.

At this point, he should discover that the glove will always be in the scent path, and if he strays from the path, he will lose the scent. When he has achieved success to this point, you are ready to extend your track . . . after he is able to go out seventy-five or one hundred yards, he is ready to make his first turn.

Turn stakes, preferably thirty-six to forty-eight inch green bamboo plant stakes available at most floral and landscaping shops, are now needed. Their important purpose is to visually mark the turning points for the handler or tracklayers who are at a distance . . . for nothing can confuse a dog more than to be told he is wrong when he is right. In this way, he knows exactly where he should turn.

The track should face the wind and be about fifty yards long. Pushing your bamboo turnstakes into the ground an arm's length from this mark, make a ninety degree turn, either to the right or left, and count out about fifteen yards. Having dropped the glove, retrace your steps and send the dog after it. When he comes to the turning point, he will run out of scent; encourage him to look for it. As he circles and *CASTS* for the new scent path, watch him closely.

There will be a noticeable characteristic *SIGNAL* given by the dog. It may be a change in head position, or even tail position; watch closely for it, since he'll do it every time when searching for the track. When he finds the new track he'll give another signal. Encourage him and lavish praise on him when he finds the new track, but especially when he finds the glove, for he has really accomplished something!

You have now reached the point where retracing your steps may start to confuse the dog, therefore, after dropping the glove, continue onward in a straight line for at least fifty feet. At this point, any turn can cause the dog to miss the glove, since he may short-cut to the new leg, due to wind conditions, and miss the glove completely.

Outlined, so far, is probably several weeks' work or more, as you must be sure not to tire or bore your dog. While working Blitzen one Sunday morning in August, it suddenly grew very hot, and becoming overheated little Blitzen just quit. It took over two years of hard work to get her to start tracking again, so that she could earn her T. She would go out and then simply decide that she had had enough and that would be it for the day. In her first tracking test, she walked three steps past the second flag, and decided to call it a day . . . was I embarrassed! She earned her T the next year, just six weeks before her tenth birthday. There is no way to force your dog if he does not want to track, but when he wants to track then it's a real pleasure. Most Dachshunds work close to the center of the scent path, but a few seem to like to work the edge, or fringe, and work back to the base path.

Aging the track is your next step in training. One waits about ten minutes before putting the dog on track and continuously extends the waiting periods, until the dog can work a two hour old track. After he can do a thirty minute old track, you come to the next step, the Transfer Track, where a friend follows in your footsteps as you lay the track, and drops the glove. After a short wait, put the dog on the combined track. Although he may be confused at first, with the proper encouragement he'll proceed till he finds the glove, and then should realize what's going on.

After a lot of praise, have your friend lay a short track and drop the glove. Be sure he knows exactly what to do . . . I have found it safest to use the turn stakes, as it takes a lot of practice to know exact locations in a great big empty field. Eventually start using your friends and neighbors to lay track, extending the track until it is 500 yards long, aged to two hours and having a half-dozen turns in it. Remember not to push your dog too fast or too long, for if he gets bored, you will then have a devil of a time getting him interested again.

Some tracking experts never put the dog on their own track, but start using a stranger from the very first. The advantage of using your own track is that you can work any time you are ready and not have to depend on someone else having some spare time at the right time. On the way home, I'd lay a track in some fields near our house, and after changing clothes, I would take the dog out and put him on an aged track of half hour or more. Unfortunately, not all of us have this advantageous surrounding.

I strongly advocate the use of turn stakes for a good long time, unless you are fortunate to have experienced tracklayers to work with, since there is nothing more frustrating than to get out in the field and have your track-layer say, "I think the turn is somewhere around here." I, therefore, have made it a security habit to use a little notebook with sketches of the track, noting the landmarks ahead, behind and to the side.

When your dog can follow an aged track of 500 yards with no markers other than the two starting flags, and you have reached the point where you can "read" his signals, you are ready to find a tracking judge and ask for a certification test. You will find the judges most obliging, in helping your dog *EARN* his certification. Once you have this certification, valid for a period of six months, all you have to do is find a Tracking Test, send your entry blank in with the certification and then *GOOD LUCK*.

THE DACHSHUND AS A HUNTING DOG!!

By David C. Mullen, Jr.

(D.C.A.'s Field Trial Chairman for the past 11 years; third Vice-President of D.C.A. for the past four years; Director of the Western Pennsylvania D.C.)

Have you ever thought of taking that little adorable pet Dachshund, you are holding on your lap, outdoors and letting him get acquainted with the marvelous scents that can be found in the fields or wooded areas? Do you really want to deprive him of the pleasure of seeking and trailing game?

The great nose, that the Dachshund possesses, makes him a potential rabbit trailer, and also helps him drive squirrels to trees or to rout pheasants.

In training a Dachshund for the field, you do not have to complicate matters with too many commands. If your dog will come to you on command and knows the meaning of "No," you have completed most of the training. The rest can only be accomplished by frequent visits to the great outdoors, where the strong hunting instinct usually takes over.

If you have an older dog that shows an interest in hunting rabbits, it will make it easier to train a puppy (the younger the better). By taking them both out together, the puppy will stay with and imitate the older dog. Eventually, the puppy will be in position to get the scent of the rabbit being chased and will enter into the fun of the chase.

Live trapped rabbits can be put to good use. After showing and teasing the Dachshund with the rabbit, so that he associates the scent with the animal, release it in a field, giving the rabbit a good start. The puppy should be able to start trailing it by using that good nose he possesses.

Field Trial Champion Jay of Da-Dor with owner David C. Mullen of Pennsylvania. Photo by Howard Morse.

One of the charming drawings by Dot Mullen which accompanied the announcement of the forthcoming D.C.A. Field Trial.

In search of a "Tallyho," the cry of the huntsman on first sighting the game. First Sanctioned Field Trial of the Dachshund Club of New Jersey, Spring, 1967. Among the group are one of the judges, Dr. H. E. Adler (center), and Barry P. Adler, who acts as a "beater" to flush the game (far right). Photo by Leonore Loeb Adler.

The judges in conference: Dr. Helmut E. Adler (left) and Mr. Lloyd Bowers (right). Photo by Leonore L. Adler.

The judges, the committee members, the winners and some workers at the First A.K.C. Sanctioned Field Trial of the D.C.N.J. (Not all people present were identified.) Front row from left: George S. Wanner, president of the club; Mrs. George S. Goodspeed (center) whose Ch. Cyrano's Plume of Greenfield was Best in Trial; and Mr. Jeanneney, holding a ribbon, whose Carla vom Rode was the Winner among the bitches. Back row from left: Mrs. Charles W. Campbell, field trail secretary; Mr. C. W. Campbell, chairman field trial committee; Mr. Lloyd Bowers, judge; and Dr. Helmut E. Adler, judge. Photo by Leonore L. Adler.

Along the trail of D.C.A.'s 44th Annual Field Trial: Brace on Rabbit. Photo by George C. Wanner.

Ric-Ran's Wee Waggie Maggie, a smooth Miniature bitch, won not only the Open All-Age Bitch Stakes, but also the Open All-Age Winner of the Absotlue Brace on Rabbit (the equivalent to Best of Winners at conformation dog shows). This was the first time that a Miniature won top honors! Left, William Stephenson, father of Robert Stephenson, owner; center, Emma Jean (Mrs. William) Stephenson, handler; and right, Mrs. Leonore Loeb Adler, chairman of the D.C.A.'s Miniature Dachshund Committee. Photo by Dr. Helmut E. Adler. (One year after this picture was taken, Maggie became the first Miniature Dachshund Field Trial Champion at the 45th Annual Field Trial of D.C.A.)

You are now on your way to having a hunting Dachshund. The proficiency of your dog will now depend on the frequency of your visits to your training area.

The qualifications to look for in your Dachshunds are a good nose, which most of them are blessed with, courage in facing heavy thickets where rabbits like to seek shelter, perseverance, keenness and the determination to go to earth without hesitation.

All field trials are run under the Rules of the American Kennel Club. Permission is obtained by a club to hold such a trial by writing to the A.K.C., giving date, location and judges. After permission is granted by the A.K.C. to hold the Field Trial, the club appoints a field trial secretary, who must be approved by the A.K.C. Then a field trial committee must be appointed, who is responsible for conducting the trial. The committee must have at least five members of the club.

Two months before the trial is held, two copies of a Questionnaire Form (supplied by A.K.C.) are distributed with: date; exact location; all details of stakes to be run (Dachshunds have only two regular stakes—Open All Age Dogs (Singles) and Open All Age Bitches (Singles) and a Non-Regular Stake "For Champions Only"); all money and prizes the club wishes to offer; names and addresses of the two judges; names and addresses of club officers; field trial secretary's name and address; name and address of the chairman of the trial and names of all other members of the field trial committee; the date, hour and place of closing of the entries and the date, hour and place of the drawing of the entries. After the field trial secretary receives all entries, the drawing of braces can take place.

Each dog or bitch entered must be at least six months old and registered in the A.K.C. All entries must be completed in full! Entries will be accepted from any person in good standing with the A.K.C. No experience on part of owner or dog is needed and everyone enjoys the day in the field with their Dachshunds. There have been many first time entered Dachshunds who have won their stake.

Dogs not entered in the trial will not be permitted on the field trial grounds. Any dog, entered and present at a field trial, must compete in all stakes in which it is entered, unless excused by the field trial committee, after reaching this decision by consulting with the judges.

Two judges are used at Dachshund field trials and their decision, on the winners in each stake, is decided by running all braces in each stake, and then having a second series of run-offs of the two or more dogs or bitches considered to have the highest points. Occasionally, third and fourth series of run-offs are needed to arrive at the winners.

The four highest scoring dogs and bitches are awarded ribbons and the fifth dog and bitch is considered as NBQ (next best qualifying). Only the first and second place winners receive points toward their championships. First place dog and bitch receive one (1) point for each dog or bitch competing against them and the second place dog and bitch receive one-third the number of points of the winner, provided there are nine (9) or more actual starters. To complete a Field Championship, a dog or bitch must have at least one first place win.

Only trials that are run with live cottontails or hares are permitted to carry Championship Points. At the present time it takes a total of twenty-five points for a Dachshund to be recorded a Field Champion.

Nowadays there are three (3) point field trials held for Dachshunds in the United States. The Dachshund Club of America, Inc., being the oldest, will hold its 46th Annual Field Trial in 1972. The Dachshund Club of New Jersey, Inc., held its sixth A.K.C. licensed Trial the same year and Connecticut Yankee Dachshund Club also had a licensed A.K.C. Field Trial in 1971. Another Trial took place in early 1972 by the Western Pennsylvania Dachshund Club, Inc. It is hoped that more clubs will follow suit, giving Dachshunds a chance to do the work in the field for which they were originally bred.

DACHSHUND RACING

By Wini and Rod MacLean
(Treasurer of the Springfield, Oregon, Kennel Club)

and Mary Lou Hatcher
(Director of the same kennel club, as well as licensed professional handler.)

Dachshund racing got off to a fast and exciting start in the West when the Whippet Coursing Club invited members of the Dachshund Obedience Club of Los Angeles to join them for a day of racing . . . probably feeling the Dachshunds would be hilarious. However, the little guys fooled everyone and took to chasing the lure like pros.

Nearly thirty Dachshunds, Miniature and Standard, showed up the first day and many turned out to be naturals . . . greatly impressing the Whippet owners who often have to train their dogs to chase.

Dogs and people had such a good time, in fact, that we soon developed a lure-pulling device of our own . . . and then went on to such sophisticated (but unnecessary) things as a starting box, colorful racing coats and flags to outline the course.

For the Dachshunds who do not take an immediate interest in the lure, which is usually a fox, raccoon tail or a piece of rabbit fur, we find that a little "teasing" with the lure will often bring them around. By letting the

The Starting Box is opened by Barbara Haisch of California, while Rod MacLean of Oregon operates the lure-pulling device for racing track. The course is outlined by flags. Photo by Wini Mac Lean.

reluctant ones play with the lure, and then using it in a cat-and-mouse type of game, they are often inspired to try to catch it . . . especially when another dog is allowed to start chasing it first.

Frequently, the handler of the lure-pulling device will underestimate the speed of the Dachshunds and they will catch the lure . . . thus necessitating having extra tails on hand. These fierce little chasers can pull a fox tail or rabbit skin to shreds in a remarkably short time!

Races are held in heats of two or four dogs . . . going only to the end of the course and being caught there by their handlers or going the entire distance, down and back. We separate Miniatures and Standards for the heats . . . ending with a race among all the winners . . . and often a mini is the grand winner.

For spectators, a free-for-all, about ten racers let go together, is an

Fancy, one of the Running Dog Ranch Miniature Dachshund racing team member, is followed by that ear-flapping, swift Swede, Pummel. The owner of the Dachshunds is Wini MacLean. Wini and Rod MacLean and Mary Lou Hatcher all of Oregon are partners in the ranch. Photo by Rod MacLean.

exciting moment . . . but this should be tried only with experienced dogs so as not to frighten any of them.

Soon after we started "racing," local kennel clubs, hearing of the races, invited us to put on exhibitions . . . thereby grew "Dachshund racing" in the West. Since then, the races have been a high spot at many A.K.C. shows and matches. They are entertaining, hilarious and colorful; and enjoyed by all.

For those interested in trying their hand at racing, the building of a lure is relatively simple. (See Fig. 1.) We built ours from a clamp-on grinder . . . substituting a large movie reel for the grinding wheel. This was mounted on a collapsible sawhorse. At the other end of the approximately one hundred foot course, another sawhorse is set up with a bicycle wheel attached to the top so that it can still rotate. (See Fig. 2.) The line (the first we used was fifty pound nylon test from Rod's marlin reel) goes continuously around the movie reel and the bicycle wheel . . . enabling the lure to be pulled completely around the course or back and forth, as necessary, to keep it away from the dogs.

Fig. 1.

TOP VIEW OF
RACING SET-UP.

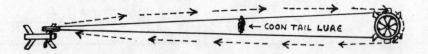

← COON TAIL LURE

The Whippet people used a lure that went in only one direction, therefore, before each race the lure would have to be walked back to the starting line. We, being lazier by nature, find that our circular course is more successful.

If the races are held out of doors, the sawhorses should be staked to the ground with tent pegs and rope to keep them from toppling over when the dogs catch the lure.

One word of caution . . . watch your fingers when retrieving the lure as these Dachshunds, when fired up, don't seem to care whether someone's fingers are attached to the lure or not!

Fig. 2. RACING EQUIPMENT

A. SAWHORSE with grinder attachment; grinding wheel replaced by empty movie reel.

B. BICYCLE WHEEL for lure to go around and return.

C. DECORATION TO OUTLINE COURSE (flags or multi-colored triangles.

D. RACING COAT (colored felt)

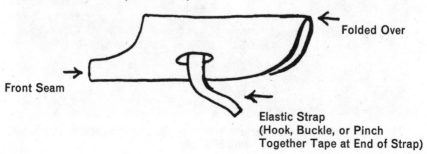

Folded Over

Front Seam

Elastic Strap
(Hook, Buckle, or Pinch
Together Tape at End of Strap)

Fancy outruns his racing partner to victory—lure in foreground. Photo by
Rod MacLean.

The undisputed captain of the racing team is Running D's Little Harvey,
here shown as a puppy. Owner Wini MacLean of Oregon. Photo by Rod
and Wini MacLean.

Ch. Jiridox Jujube, owned and loved by Peggy Westphal.
Photo by William P. Gilbert.

A LOVABLE DACHSHUND★

By BEVERLY SHARMAINE ADLER

A sight I see is a Dachshund
　　　　　licking his master,
Now I see, he's licking
　　　　　even faster.
He's a lovable Dachshund,
　　　　　lovable indeed,
He's what anyone would want,
　　　　　anyone would need!

* *Reprinted with permission from the* N.M.D.C. Miniature Dachshund Digest,
October, 1967, p. 11.

EPILOGUE

We have arrived at the end of our consideration of the Dachshund. Possibly the reader may feel differently about certain of the subjects covered; but it is hoped that he has gained the impression that the author's pen was moved by the love for the Dachshund and concern about his future.

Like a continuous thread, running through the book, there is the hope to preserve the Dachshund with all his endowments. May all to whom the future of the Dachshund is entrusted employ their best energy to preserve his artistically perfect form, which abhors any exaggeration and retain, above all, his mental alertness, and his physical fitness.

For you, "Dachsie," and for your future path through life, may you, for many centuries, delight the hearts of your friends!

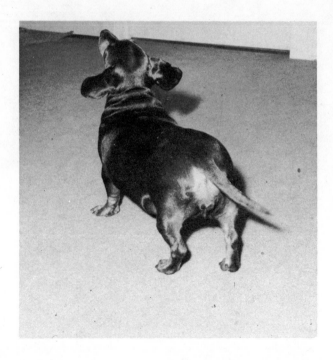

INDEX

T

U

V

W

Z